Christian Identity on Campus

OTHER CHURCH AND CAMPUS BOOKS

Published in collaboration with
The Church Society for College Work

Community on Campus
Multi-Media Worship

Christian
Identity
on Campus

edited by Myron B. Bloy, Jr.

 THE SEABURY PRESS · NEW YORK

Published in collaboration with The Church Society for College Work

ACKNOWLEDGMENTS

Grateful acknowledgment is made to the following publishers for permission to use the specified copyrighted material:

Chapter 3: Excerpt from Daniel P. Moynihan, "Nirvana Now," in *The American Scholar,* Autumn 1967.

Chapter 5: Lines from "Anecdote of the Jar," by Wallace Stevens in *The Collected Poems of Wallace Stevens* (New York: Alfred A. Knopf, Inc., 1967); copyright 1923 and renewed 1951 by the author.

Chapter 5: Excerpt from Nikos Kazantzakis, *The Odyssey: A Modern Sequel* (New York: Simon and Schuster, 1958); copyright 1958 by Simon and Schuster.

Chapter 5: Poetry of Rainer Maria Rilke from *Duino Elegies,* translated by J. B. Leishman and Stephen Spender (New York: W. W. Norton and Company, 1939); copyright 1939 by W. W. Norton and Company, Inc.; copyright renewed, 1967, by Stephen Spender and J. B. Leishman.

Contents

Editor's Introduction

THESE papers address themselves to the question of the *identity* of Christians because the world today is the scene of such epochal change that the stability and coherence of our *selves,* and not just the constructs of our minds, is threatened. During relatively stable stretches of history men can, like jugglers, gain the necessary confidence and skill to keep a myriad of pretty ideas dancing in the air. Many intellectuals, including theologians, even experience a kind of self-forgetful joy in playing that game. But today we find it impossible to concentrate on our juggling because the ground is shifting under our very feet; we now must give urgent attention to saving our selves from the ancient threat of chaos while simultaneously forging new identities commensurate with the emerging new world. We are, in short, beginning to discover that the integrity of our selves, not merely our airy ideas, is at stake.

In fact, the most important thing to say about this nation in this time is that it is undergoing a profound spiritual crisis. The terms in which the crisis is manifested and by which it is precipitated are political, technological, and economic, but its deepest reality is nonetheless spiritual. That is, the underlying assumptions about the ultimate nature of man on which we built our social order are themselves up for grabs and not merely the order itself. The last time we faced such a crisis was in the Civil War, and just as that war represented for the nation both the threat of chaos and the hope of a new spiritual creation, so does this new crisis. For us, the threat of chaos comes from the collapse—in ability to fulfill its ends as well as in the moral integrity of those ends—of the liberal, technocratic world-view. And our hope—nurtured largely by a visionary youth culture—is for a more whole, sentient, and morally responsible life.

This crisis of fear and hope is nowhere more clearly felt than on the campus where it has precipitated a passionate quest for a new life—for, in the words of St. Paul, "a new creation." In this situation, intellectual inquiry takes on a certain gutsy quality that is usually lacking in academic culture. The more sensitive students and faculty seem to be trying to break through the neat intellectual proprieties of their rationalistic world in order to discover a deeper, more stable, and more satisfying reality. In fact, they seem, implicitly or explicitly, to be possessed by that same "ontological obsession," that same passion to discover and live deeply in the mystery and power of being itself, which characterized primitive religious man and by which he held chaos at bay.

Although the need of a deeper grounding and more coherent identity for the self is felt by most sensitive people on campus, it has an especially poignant quality for Christians. Christians are, after all, those who formally claim a gospel that provides precisely that grounding and identity; yet they are as shaken as anyone else by the new threat and promise. We Christians have, in fact, been caught playing the same effete, intellectual games as everyone else, and the discovery of this ironic situation is frightening to ourselves and debilitating to our ostensible mission. For example, students' interest in religion is no longer confined to delicate skirmishes over such matters as the possibility of a virgin birth; but, rather, they demand with burning eyes to be led—by mystic vision and moral passion—into the presence of the Holy One Himself. Obviously, no mere "scribe" can lead that trip, but only one with "authority," one with a coherent spiritual identity. For most campus Christians, such identity has long since been distorted and diluted by the now collapsing academic culture. Administrators and faculty, formerly so sleek and self-assured as priests of the academic culture, are now severely shaken by a crisis of professional and personal identity which plunges them into the deepest questions of meaning and purpose. Again, most campus Christians are themselves so uncertain of their own identity that they can offer little help in responding to the danger and opportunity of this spiritual crisis.

What, then, is a Christian identity that is responsive to the current spiritual upheaval centered on the campus? The Church Society for College Work invited seven campus Christians to work together to provide some answers to that question. They wrote preliminary papers, then met together for nearly a week on an island off the coast of Maine to test each paper for its adequacy; later each rewrote his paper in the light of that testing. The place we met—the house of rough timbers and boards, of massive stone chimneys and hearths, grounded on the island's headland with its deck cantilevered over the crashing sea and backed to a whispering spruce forest—was itself an invitation to entertain the mystery of existence. This setting achieved paradigmatic power when, newly arrived from, and still conditioned by, the rationalistic, competitive, tight-assed world of the university, we sailed in a whistling wind out to see a sea-hawk's nest on another lonely island. As we approached the nest with sails slatting, the two hawks, mates, rose screaming fiercely to protect their young. As they hung above us, our mouths and minds and hearts opened to receive the mystery, establishing the depth of our encounter with each other and with our task for the following days. That night we read, by kerosene lamp and firelight, Richard Eberhart's "Sea-Hawk," symbol for him of the "permanence of the impersonal," and were reminded again of Gerard Manley Hopkins' "Windhover," for

Hopkins the very image of Christ's glory and power, of the permanence of the *personal*. The hawk became for the consultants the symbolic entrance into that dimension of reality where real identity is grounded. As a result, we believe the reader will discover in these papers a deeper, more adventurous, even more authentic grappling with Christian identity in our time than could be expected from the usual academic exercise. Here, we hope, are imaginative probes which will provide rich agenda for the serious reflection of all Christians at this critical moment.

I

William McAuliffe:

"Jesus' own ultimate confirmation of identity depended on no ethnic, ritualistic, or legalistic little world; not even upon the secular world or upon physical life. It depended only upon his relationship to his Father: 'And I am not alone, because the Father is with me.'"

PERSONAL identity develops in dialogue and interaction between oneself and the world. Subjectively, it is belief about whom one has become and what his purpose is: "I can say this about myself." Personality theorists speak of self-esteem, or identity, in terms of the verbal artifice we build around ourselves in order to cope with the anxieties of "making it" in the process of human living. I need a symbolic self-understanding. I also need the world to respond supportively to what I believe myself to be. So my search for self-confirmation becomes a continuing struggle to play a role in which I can speak myself to the world and hear the reply, "You are O.K. You function well." The problem today is that in man's present surroundings the old identity-fashioning devices are becoming rapidly extinct.

I recall my smug identity when, as a confident young sailor, my world was a navy ship and its crew. I knew all the men, my job, how to respond effectively to any emergency. Identity in this little realm was no large problem. The strangest ports held little fear for me because my "world" was tied up in the harbor nearby. I was certain that any venture into chaos ashore could end safely with my return aboard. But today such safe havens have a frighteningly miragelike way of disappearing. Tight little worlds like ships, towns, clubs, churches, countries, loyalties, sects, time-honored traditions, dogmatic systems, even families, have lost their protective mystique. We see and hear too much from beyond them to be deluded into thinking that they alone can confirm our self-beliefs.

Small wonder that we seek new expressions for *Christian* identity now that the man-made social and creedal constructs built to confirm it are breaking down. Perhaps at last we are being forced not to attempt any further Christian belief bases less extensive than our deepest understandings of man and history themselves. In my opinion there would be much less of a problem of Christian identity today had we not done to Christianity over and over again the same disservice that Jesus implicitly criticized his own people for doing to Judaism. That is, reducing the message-in-history to excessive dependency upon sheltering, closed-ended systems. The result in Christianity has been the replacement of the universalizing, identity-building power of Christianity by cultural, institutional, and rubrical constructs with a creeping tendency to become false absolutes in their own right.

What, then, can be said of "Christian identity"—that concept of selfhood which draws upon the gospel for its validity? Certainly it cannot be separated from personal identity. A Christian is a man like any other, who depends for his self-confirmation upon how he meets the world around him and how it feeds back to him; whose identity is a form of *belief:* what he believes himself and the world to be. Here is the point where I see the place for *Christian* identity. The Christian humanist scarcely differs functionally from the non-Christian humanist in terms of self-sacrifice to a world future beyond his own. He *is* different, nonetheless. He chooses to identify with a tradition which seeks its meaning in the relationship of life, death, human community, and history to the death and resurrection of Jesus Christ. But today's seriously thinking Christian finds this relationship increasingly difficult to establish in the conventional theological frameworks and language. In his search for relevancy he is tempted to depart from old forms of expression entirely, salvaging only the "Christian" label. Even that label has become discomforting for some, and they prefer the term *"post*-Christian." But I would insist that the would-be post-Christian consider the possibility of resources in the New Testament death-resurrection paradigm not yet sufficiently explored. When I raise this point with colleagues I am asked to explain why, really, one need be so insistent. Must I try dutifully to squeeze my world-view under a "Christian" umbrella only because I *happen to be* a Christian and want to stay loyal—perhaps also because, since I am a clergyman, my livelihood depends on keeping alive "Christianity" with a capital C? Or rather, is there an enduring, unique value-frame in Christian revelation which affords special meaning all its own? I am compelled to hold that there is, because I understand that the existence of such a value-frame is implicit in Christian tradition itself.

Either one takes the New Testament seriously as a call to a communicable belief-commitment to a self-transforming way of living vis-à-vis God and man, or else one must face honestly the question as to whether "Christian identity" is sufficiently definable to discuss. To me the whole issue of Christian identity is this confronting. But to talk this way is to invite upon oneself the challenge of announcing the inherent relevancy of Christianity to contemporary man. How can this be done? There seems to be no widely accepted conceptual set and language for bridging the Christ paradigm to man's concrete historic present. I believe that this problem of bridging is closely related to what Richard Underwood describes in his chapter as the need for a theology reaching to the enduring "arche" beneath the veneers of dogmatic language. If, as Underwood's quote from Jung says, "Inside [man] reign the archaic gods, supreme as of old," and if Christianity can speak credibly of unity of men in the Spirit, somehow these fundamental concepts must converge in the same reality. What other than this assumption could have stirred Paul to speak as he did to the men of Athens? The Father of Jesus Christ and the Athenians' "unknown God" were one and the same. Are we being too reckless to imagine Paul speaking similarly to *homo religiosus* today?

Perhaps no one has probed the transcendental depths of man's existence more articulately than Paul Tillich. In an article

"Counter-Culture and Academic Reform," [1] Myron Bloy explores Tillich's notion of "self-transcending realism" as a way for "uncovering and breaking through the current impasse between the academic and counter-cultures." Tillich proposed self-transcending realism as a way of *faith:* one experiences the "really real" in a concrete historic moment by clasping the paradox of both its transient and its eternal aspects. To do so is to *believe.* Bloy quotes Tillich: "The ultimate power of being, the ground of reality, appears in a special moment, in a concrete situation, revealing the infinite depth and the eternal significance of the present. But this is possible only in terms of paradox, i.e., faith, for in itself, the present is neither infinite nor eternal. . . . When reality is seen this way with the eye of self-transcending realism, it has become something new. Its ground has become visible in an 'ecstatic' experience, called 'faith.' "

I share Bloy's expectations for the usefulness of Tillich's approach, not only for breaking through the epistemological barriers between academic and counter-cultures, but also for establishing avenues of understanding between conventional and counter-traditional modes of religious belief. Today's youth counter-culture, with its bewildering variety of manifestations on campus and off, reaches singular accord in its admiration of what appears as "real," "honest," "beautiful," "right on." It has, too, a strong savor for experiencing the transcendent in concrete moments. Witness the recent popularity of Robert A. Heinlein's *Stranger in a Strange Land,* with his unworldly power to "grok," i.e., intuit the mysterious core of persons and events. I see these tendencies in youth as a groping for "ground" or "arche" in life experience, relatable to the insights explored by men such as Tillich and Jung. Buber speaks of "Thou"; Jesus of "Father." In our context of Christian identity, the question is whether the valid transcending experiences of all cultures, including today's youth counter-culture, are identifiable with what the New Testament sees as fundamental in the death and resurrection of Jesus, and how, for the Christian at least, the New Testament approach can offer unique relevance. But in order even to pose this question, it seems to me that the Christian death-resurrection paradigm must be reassessed.

The secularist turn of contemporary American Christian theology has moved toward a reassessment. Yet when it comes close it often takes on the aspects of an aircraft shuddering in the midst of the sonic barrier without shooting through to clear flight on the other side. The reverberations come in increasingly labored theo-philosophizings which offer little to the everyday business of shaping a usable Christian view in the revolutionary world. The result is often not a breakthrough but a breakoff; not a secularized *theo*logy at all, but only humanism pure and simple, handled with a kind of nostalgia for traditional Christian expressions that led us up to the impasse but didn't help us through. We talk about war, poverty, and technological enslavement with a nod back to "Christianity," while others seem to do just as well nodding only to each other.

Can we break through to the other side? Can Christian identity survive in a new form once old handles are let go? I believe so. But the breakthrough may require a more risky and even reckless exploration of the New Testament theme than we have indulged in up to now.

At the risk of oversimplification and, perhaps, heresy, I would suggest that the life, death, and resurrection of Jesus "saved" man not simply by being an "act of reparation" or a new corrective intervention of God's efficacious power into human history; rather, it was the revelation of the dynamic, creative, evolutionary *relationship* which has *always* existed between God and man, but heretofore only vaguely and primitively understood. "He was in the world that had its being through him, and the world did not know him" (John 1:10). Jesus' responsible confrontation with his life-death crisis was the climax of his earthly relationship to his "Father." As such, it became the model for man's own finding of a relationship with God nowhere but in history itself. This was no transmission of a plurality of "doctrines" to disciples to be "handed down." It was the paradigm for seeing human life and death as mystery, communication, and response—that is, prayer *par excellence.* It patterns man's mature relationship to the personal fundament of his history, past, present, and future. "The spirit you received is not the spirit of slaves bringing fear into your lives again, it is the spirit of sons, and it makes us cry out, 'Abba, Father!' The Spirit himself and our spirit bear united witness that we are children of God. And if we are children we are heirs as well: heirs of God and coheirs with Christ, sharing his sufferings so as to share his glory" (Rom. 8:15–17). To be "baptized into his death" (Rom. 6:4) is to grasp one's own realization of that co-responsibility with the "Father" to which Jesus gave himself for the future reconciliation of man.

In his journey to the cross, Jesus engaged in a death struggle against the enslaving human power systems of his own time. To read the Gospels seriously without seeing him as a radical and reformer is hardly possible. His strife to "set the down-trodden free" (Luke 4:18) denounced all who would use power to exploit others for self-gain. It took him to the midst of death, but there he found "life." His own ultimate confirmation of identity depended on no ethnic, ritualistic, or legalistic "little world"; not even upon the secular world or upon physical life. It depended only upon his relationship to his "Father": "And I am not alone, because the Father is with me" (John 16:3).

"Going to the Father" was for Jesus not a passage *out* of the world, but into its very "ground" in the Tillichean sense—into headlong confrontation with its *life,* even unto death. In reflection upon this death-to-life transitus the Church community achieves the resurrection view which becomes its exemplar of all human hope. "Blessed be God the Father of our Lord Jesus Christ, who in his great mercy has given us a new birth as his sons, by raising Jesus Christ from the dead, so that we may have a sure hope . . ." (I Pet. 1:3). The death-resurrection view might be stated thus: To come to grips with the challenge of our human existence is to confront "death": the risky, the dark, and the unknown. But to move into it nevertheless—to pass into death for the sake of one's convictions, is, in fact, to *live* most fully. "We believe that having died with Christ we shall return to life with him" (Rom. 6:8). Jesus meets his Father in the midst of death and so finds "life." What appeared in human perspective as the most feared and desolate prospect turned out to be the narrow gate into the depths of reality and encounter with God.

Lest this view appear too death-centered, as though the Christian ideal is a search for the difficult, I would insist that it is quite the opposite. The entire theme of Jesus' public life is the effort to bestow life and happiness, "to bring good news to the poor, to proclaim liberty to captives, to the blind new sight" (Luke 4:18). Nonetheless, in the condition man finds himself to be in, such a struggle necessarily operates in tension with the inertia of the self-centered material world, that is, "death." The "saving" factor of the Christian view is precisely belief that in direct wrestling with the death-dealing forces one in fact does not die, but *lives* most fully. "He who would save his life will lose it; but he who loses his life for my sake will find it" (Matt. 16:25). This life struggle, reminiscent of Jacob's wrestling, is the price of creative encounter with the personal source and end of human existence—the Thou, the Father who alone ensures response to the identity-search of man.

If this attempt to apply the death-resurrection theme of the

New Testament to human life seems unrealistic, I would attempt to illustrate that it is borne out experientially in nearly every real human drama. My favorite example is the simple life-situation of confronting another person on a hard-to-discuss matter of personal concern to oneself and the other. For a long time I have masked my true feelings from my friend and skirted a difficult issue. But the "hour comes" when I decide I must deal with it. The effort is painful. I risk the "death" of my friend's misunderstanding, perhaps even the loss of his friendship. But I do risk nevertheless, and pass through the "death." In this particular instance we reach an understanding, and the issue is resolved between us. Instead of ending in death, my honest plunge brings us together in deeper friendship than before: resurrection. A small example, but I believe it speaks of every interpersonal, communal, and creative effort in human life— even though in some situations the "resurrection experience" is not as immediately apparent as in others.

Christ's death is considered an overcoming of "sin." A familiar contemporary understanding of sin is the refusal to live fully by one's convictions and to be as much as possible one's authentic self to others. It is a flight from responsibility to self and the world—an avoidance of growth, or to use Erich Fromm's phrase, an "escape from freedom." As such, sin is an "affront to God" (to return to traditional parlance) precisely because it is an *affront to life*. Sin is the refusal to engage the perceived opportunities of existence. And certainly it is in man's coping with existence that he must meet God, if indeed there *is* a personal ground of existence and if he meets man at all. In Paul's words Christ "died to sin." He endured the death of engaging the full responsibilities of his existence rather than submit to the "sin" of avoiding them. His journey to the cross is the paradigm of overcoming the temptation to be less than authentically human; his resurrection the sign that such a choice is indeed "life saving." The Christian, according to Paul, "dies daily." But this death is also resurrection. And baptism signifies the Christian's awareness of this belief: "You have been taught that when we were baptized in Christ Jesus we were baptized into his death. . . . If in union with Christ we have imitated his death, we shall also imitate him in his resurrection" (Rom. 6:3,5).

Like Jesus, I meet God my Father directly in engagement with my life in the world. I believe that I love and am loved by the Father in the depths of life and death themselves. But this is magnificently good news! News to be thankful (eucharistic) for—news to be danced and sung! The celebrating together by those who believe and enact it becomes in turn a more profound insight into its meaning. Thus the "word" becomes sacramentalized, uniquely incarnate, in that community we know as the "church."

In this renewed expression of belief I no longer find consolation in the thought that I might *pray to* Jesus, or that Jesus is somehow "in me" or standing by me. The New Testament account of him as Risen Lord gives new testimony to the powers of *man*. If Jesus is standing by me, he does so in the presence of other men. If I want to speak to him, whether to help or ask for help, I will dialogue with the men and institutions of the world. Then what of his "Father"? To find him I will look not *away from* my life and death experience, but *into* it, *with a sensitivity to its transcendent mystery*. When his disciples asked about the whereabouts of his Father, Jesus asked how it was he could be with them so long without their realizing "he who sees me sees the Father" (John 14:9). Have I been in the world so long and have not experienced its Spirit, its mystery? As a Christian can I not be mystical enough to believe that my very experience of the world, its good and evil, its life and death, is in fact my experience of God—my honest response to its challenges my honest response to him?

The recent emphases on "nonverbal experience" in forms of group encounter teach that person-to-person communication is far more than only a matter of words. But a deep sensitivity to this fact is hard to achieve. We have become so word-bound that we are uncomfortable with communicative signs unless we can easily translate what they "say" into words. But so many "messages," as in the arts, are untranslatable. So also with the full range of communication between one person and another. Perhaps really secularized, breakthrough Christianity will come about only when we become more willing to let *God* reach us in *his* own signs—the signs of our world situation, without our feeling the need to mythologize or apotheosize them. The most profound message of Scripture may be just this: God meets man in history. But we strain so hard to unravel the "message" that perhaps we tend to forget the messaging. I mean that we may get so caught up in attempts to decipher *what* God has revealed that we overlook the possibility that he *is* interacting with us constantly, nonverbally—calling men to create their way into his future in engaging the oncoming crises of social and world development. Indeed—if the world is the medium of God-man encounter, to what extent is it also the message?

Arend van Leeuwen, in his *Prophecy in a Technocratic Era,* says that the fundamental concern of our Christian existence in the world is *prophecy:* "the crucial distinction is neither between clergy and laity, or between theology and secular science, or between mission and service, but between *prophetic* and *unprophetic* theology, laity, mission, service, etc." [2] Van Leeuwen sees the two indispensable characteristics of prophecy to be (1) that it is directed toward an open future and (2) that it appeals to the possibility of conversion. "Prophecy is incompatible with any kinds of determinism." [3] The Christian prophet is able to view the future not only in terms of its limitless secular possibilities, but also as deepening relationship with the "Father." The future offers hope to him. The possibility of conversion that the Christian extends to others, in its broadest aspect is not, I would suggest, conversion to any "little world" of institution, sect, or loyalty. Rather, it is conversion to hope— hope founded in the belief that the death-resurrection effort to enrich the family of man is response to God's love.

What I am attempting to describe says nothing about *how* a Christian, as compared with a non-Christian, solves the problems of building the future world. I believe that the "how" is not Christianity's primary concern. Christianity is a faith-inspired *attitude toward the world* which allows the believer to see his human existence and purpose as ultimately personal and transcendently rooted. It equips him with a prophetic vision; it shapes his motivations, but does not necessarily instruct him. It frees him to see himself and the world from the viewpoint of the mature son-come-of-age, who can say to his God, "Abba, Father." His love and concern for the world is exercised in responsibility for his Father's house and family. He sees the whole world as the Kingdom of God, and makes the fuller realization of this Kingdom a central motivation of his life.

In this context the Church would be the minimally institutionalized movement of diversified communities who share the Christian prophetic attitude, celebrate it liturgically, and approach their life-roles with deep sensitivity to human history as a creative, sacramental happening. Without attempting here to translate this view into specific applications to the ethics of war, minorities, developing nations, population, poverty, technology, and ecology, I would hope that the implications are obvious. The practical handling of these concerns is a secular task which the Christian shares with his non-Christian brothers. His solutions will not necessarily be more or less successful than another's by virtue of his being Christian. They must withstand the same pragmatic tests. Nor need they be labeled publicly as "Christian" solutions, though they are motivated by Christian value, vision, and insight.

Christian identity, then, is faith-given awareness that one really is "at home" in the world, while faced with the stark knowledge that for most men this same world is still a vale of tears and even a well of despair. It awaits re-creation, whatever the cost. "Creation still retains the hope of being freed, like us, from its slavery to decadence, to enjoy the same freedom and glory as the children of God" (Rom. 8:21). The Christian's concern for freeing the world into his vision of hope may lead him into hazardous confrontations with those who tyrannize for fear of losing their own "little worlds" on which they stake their whole identity. Such a confrontation was the Cross.

My own efforts to discuss "Christian Identity on Today's Campus" have leaned heavily, I admit, toward the personal, conceptual aspects of faith. I have said little about the ecclesial, social, and communal aspects, nor have I stressed what is very specific to the "campus." This is partly because the accompanying chapters deal with these matters, but also because I feel that the articulation of personal Christian faith in terms of New Testament themes is unnecessarily weak among Christians on the current campus scene. Many students and faculty I know are completely turned off by old Christian conceptual frameworks and haven't discovered new ones. A large number think the search not worth making. As a campus minister I think that it is, but not without a revolution in the layman's understanding of the gospel message.

1. Myron B. Bloy, Jr., "Counter-Culture and the Academic Reform," *Christianity and Crisis* 30:7 (April 27, 1970), 85–90.

2. Arend Theodoor van Leeuwen, *Prophecy in a Technocratic Era* (New York: Charles Scribner's Sons, 1968), p. 36.

3. *Ibid.*, p. 14.

II

James S. Preus:

"Of Christianity, one now asks: What is it that historic Christianity gave to us that we wish it to give to all men? and what would we rather spare other men of? What does *our* history and experience have to give, and what to receive, as it flows into the histories and destinies of other men and nations?"

TO pose the question of Christian identity on the campus invites examination of the question: Is Christian identity something fixed and definable in the abstract, so that we are merely discussing how this essential identity is affected by its peculiar university context? Or are we talking about a fluid self-understanding that shifts with time and place, and which might be quite radically different in different temporal and spatial contexts?

If we choose the first way, we are simply asking, in an ill-disguised way, what a Christian is in general. Good arguments could be made for insisting upon this approach. After all, Christianity has from early times aspired to a universal identity, an identity constituted by faith in a transcendent reality, and therefore, in essence, untouched by either time or circumstance. Christians use symbols of universality and have always aspired to achieve it; therefore, one could argue, it is proper to resist fragmentary self-definition, whether in terms of nations, denominations, sects, or universities. One will not find a special *kind* of Christian there; granted that the campus milieu is unique, the problems acute, still Christian identity is not touched at its core. For Christian identity is everywhere the same.

But it must be argued on the contrary that if personal identity is not an abstraction, then neither can Christian identity be exhausted by a dogmatic or institutional definition, true in all places alike. Nor can Christian men and women be moved about like interchangeable parts. Christian identity is a psycho-*social* reality. Put another way, there is not only a sociology of religion; there is a sociology of faith as well. That is, not merely outward forms and rites and conventions, but the inner core of faith itself, is malleable and open to the material and social conditions of existence.

Thus, different social contexts, such as the university (especially the university!) impinge deeply on the Christian dimension of identity. To be "Christian" in the university is quite a different thing, both inwardly and outwardly, from being Christian in Pine City, Minnesota. It is not that the inhabitants of the latter place are such fervent believers; on the average, I suppose, their allegiance to Christ and Church, like that of their parents, is received on authority, accepted or tolerated as something that is simply there, perhaps even appreciated. People in such communities tend still to gravitate toward churches, especially if they have children, because it seems the right thing to do. Underlying this is a sense of Christian identity constituted and supported by the vague but powerful cultural consensus: that it is good to belong to a church and a bit suspicious not to; that our culture is basically Christian; that one does not respectably raise up children illiterate in the Christian tradition; that there will always be "the Church." In short, I suspect, the faith of Pine City tends to be what medieval theologians called implicit faith.

Furthermore, what has been described in such simple terms is the faith of the Christian era, of the epoch in which such things were broadly taken for granted. However, I suspect that the Christian era may be coming to an end. If this is true, the university is the place where that momentous thing is becoming most evident. There is an emerging post-Christian attitude, or apprehension and style of life, in the universities. The university has always been a place where the heretofore implicit or unexamined faith of the student was subjected to real intellectual scrutiny. Sometimes it would be lost. But even if retained, a faith once examined can never be the same, because it can never again be merely implicit.

In former days, a lost faith at the university would customarily issue in some sort of agnosticism, atheism, or secularism—at any rate, irreligion. Losing the faith meant slipping from faith toward nothing, toward pure negation. In a social context in which Christianity is the only religious option, "un-religion" indeed seems the only alternative.

But times are changing. We are witnessing the decline of Christianity all right, but along with it other forms of authentic religiousness are emerging as real possibilities. The student interest in other religious traditions seems to me much more serious and significant than it was even five years ago.

There are broader evidences of the demise of the Christian era: for example, the general decline of the West, culturally, politically, and spiritually, and the rise of the so-called Third World; the loss of a critical mass of Christian people sufficiently committed to the specific cause of the survival of the established churches; an increasingly less convincing appeal to implicit faith (talking about the faith of the Church as though it were some-thing more than the faith of concrete, living individuals); the retreat of the churches from their traditional role as credible moral leaders in society; the inability of the theological establish-ment to help nurture religion or, on the other hand, to appro-priate such phenomena of religious renewal as might be found in society at large; the way in which Christian symbols no longer carry the mysterious power they once did. The eagerness of some political leaders to nurture the faith of the people is pain-ful evidence of the extent to which the Christian religion has been bought off (a people convinced that God is favorably at-tentive to national affairs is less likely to blame its human leaders for their folly and neglect). The defection of some of the most prophetic and perceptive American black leaders from Chris-tianity—particularly the late Malcolm X—is also a sign of these times.

Many theologians make bold to speak of the "crisis of faith" —but it is like the weather: everybody talks about it but no-body does anything about it. Conferences, pleas to begin talking again about God, even retreat to Nature will not still the crisis, which is so much a critical dimension of our transitional epoch. It may be time for some, like Abraham, to leave the old gods and set out for a new place. It is a waste of energy for theologians to wallow in guilt over the death of God—not only for themselves but, as black students have pointed out, for the cause of social justice, which needs attention more urgently than do obsolescent theological systems. Theologically, the post-Christian person need not be dragged into pure secularism but, rather, may become more open to authentic human faith and religious expression wherever it appears—whether in the church, or in Dylan's "John Wesley Harding."

Traditional Christian doctrine has it that the end of the Christian era is the end of the world. In a new way, this has a ring of truth to it. The twin threats of nuclear holocaust and ecological catastrophe, the gifts of Western Christian civilization, are perhaps reasons for its decline.

It seems likely that the faith of Pine City will continue for a time. But in the university the general and customary acceptance of all things taking place within "the years of our Lord" has passed. The university is a post-Christian place. In virtue of the reality and uniqueness of life there, a person finds himself "ahead" of historical, traditional, cultural Christianity if he imagines himself in a tradition called "history of man's religiousness" (I intend that line to be taken neutrally, and not as a new sort of *Heilsgeschichte,* as though it is the new way that leads to salvation).

Without pretending that the university has mystical or eschatological significance in the universal scheme of things, it deserves attention as religiously a more significant place to be than most. The reason is that the university is the most spiritually universal of the institutions of human society, surpassing the Western church, out of which it arose, in the breadth of its

intellectual and spiritual embrace. Its universality, small-scale
and low-key though it is, and so far lacking vision and self-consciousness, points to the growing interdependence of men world-
wide. In religion it presents an exciting challenge and possibility.

The university, as crossroads of world cultures and world
religions, not merely highlights, but actually makes concrete
and living, the increasingly relative situation of Christianity,
even in the West. It bids men of faith, or men aspiring to faith,
to find a religious identity which transcends the symbolic, metaphysical, creedal, and political limitations and possibilities of
traditional Christianity. And just as significant is the fact that
the university situation bids them consider that the old secularist
or agnostic alternative is *not* the only possible way to turn. The
less complex Christian self-consciousness of the hinterland may
be impossible here, being untrue and inadequate to the actual
state of affairs in which one must live, but now there is more
to choose than sheer "irreligion."

The identity I envision and experience in the university is on
the historical boundary between what most of us mean by Christian and post-Christian—the cultural and religious epoch into
which we seem to be moving. The religious world is opening
and must open out—just as the narrow nationalistic or "West-
ernistic" mentality must crack open. My identity is becoming
what used to be called *homo religiosus,* but one who happens
to stand with his back foot in the Christian tradition.

But can one speak of being religious-in-general, and more or
less ex-Christian, and expect to be taken seriously? As one of
my Christian friends retorted, "I'm not really interested in 'religion.' " I take it he was interested in concrete faith, in a clear
center of commitment and hope, concrete life of worship in a
community of faith and love, etc. It has often been observed,
moreover, that people start getting interested in religion when

they have lost their (or "the") faith. They are pictured as people who think, perhaps nostalgically, that religion would be a nice thing to have, despite their detachment from the inner, vital faith which comes to expression in "religion." There may be something to this. But interest in religion should not be so scornfully dismissed. *For how does one come to faith but through religion?* St. Augustine allowed as much when he observed that he would never have believed the Scriptures had it not been for the church. Religion is the sign, the symbolization of faith, and also its midwife. One should therefore allow that the searching interest in religions, or religiousness, which one witnesses in the university, is an authentic searching and hoping for a faith large enough for the era in which the human race must attempt to survive.

It is true, of course, that the discussion here is an intellectualizing of the problem, and does not arise out of sustained, concrete, and direct "religious experience"; it is, like most university thinking, based largely on the peculiarly limited sphere of experience possible in an academic community. But it reflects a real state of affairs, in my opinion—a predicament in which many people find themselves, and one that has a more epochal significance than most Westerners care to admit. One may wish, like the true believer who is not interested in "religion," to have a vivid personal Christian faith and a lively community of worship and celebration, but few people seem able to manage it. Theological language gets progressively thinner and less compelling. It may be that teachers in divinity schools are the most deeply agnostic or atheistic people in our culture. All this makes rather beside the point what one, perhaps nostalgically, *wants* to be the case.

From the perspective of its Christian rootage, the identity I describe is an identity in difficulty, having left its "home," abandoned its groping for meaning in the classic Christian faith, now engaged in search of becoming united with the faith and hope and real life of a much larger segment of mankind. This identity is shaken by the relativizing of the old faith. Of Christianity, one now asks: What is it that historic Christianity gave to us that we wish it to give to all men? and what would we rather spare other men of? What does *our* history and experience have to give, and what to receive, as it flows ever more closely into the histories and destinies of other men and nations?

This emerging sense of identity, following on the heels of a more traditional understanding of Christianity, will need to learn how to treat the Christian symbols as symbols rather than as the literal revealed or metaphysical truths handed down; how to treat them with sensitivity and respect at the same time as one weeds them out or reinterprets them in light of growing knowledge and experience and apprehension of the contemporary experience and faith of other men. It may be helpful also to re-examine decisions regarding some of Christianity's old heresies, and to rethink its crusades.

I have indicated already that "post-Christian" does not mean "secular," in the fashion of much recent theology. The so-called secular theology was fundamentally as parochial as its more traditional predecessor. For the very concept of the *saeculum* is a product of (Jewish-)Christian theology in the West. Baptizing the *saeculum* is a way of playing out the remains of that early Christian theology which invented "this (present evil) age" in the first place, and envisioned a new age to come.

The argument given here also contrasts with the Enlightenment view, insofar as that can be generalized. At that time, Europe was absorbing the impact of the discovery of the religions of the world, and at the same time reading with new eyes the classical accounts and theories of religion in general. As a result, Enlightenment thinkers came to identify the scandal and problem of Christianity as its historical particularity, and turned altogether away from history (when it came to religious norms) to "nature" as the bearer and source of authentic (because potentially universal) religiousness.

But particularity is not Christianity's problem; rather, the problem is that it tried to elevate its own history into an absolute. It called *its* history *Heilsgeschichte* and proceeded to imperialize over the histories—religious, and by implication cultural and racial—of other men. The days of Western imperialism are coming to an end, however, and the sooner Christian theology learns to withdraw ideological support from it, the better.

The trend in man's religious history should be recognized in that which is already to some extent a reality in the university: the convergence of histories and cultures and faith, East and West, the recognition of authenticity in strange religious forms, a meeting which will yield new forms of religion more universal, symbolizing and (one hopes) encouraging the drawing together of men with men into a world community of faith and action in service of the possible future of mankind.

III

Joseph Walsh:

"In the always surprising manifestations of human strength and resilience, there arises a conviction that we are not just wandering in circles in the desert, but that where we have been was to lead us to where we are now; that where we are now is *meant* to lead to some other place; that the risk of action is always a response to a true call—to the presence of His being."

THERE once was a time when we were so sure. The problem of Christian identity had been solved for us in our time, or so we thought. Caught, to begin with, in the age-old Christian dilemma between two worlds, citizen of one, resident of another, we had through Maritain, Bonhoeffer, Murray, Teilhard, and others arrived at a solution. We knew who we were. It would be our life's work only to work out what we were.

We were the bridge-builders, links between two worlds, the Church and the secular: though different and separate, the two worlds were bridgeable. They were on the same plane, in the same field; perhaps (we didn't like to think about this), one was somewhat higher than the other, but nonetheless they were joinable, linkable, passable. On that judgment our identity was based.

This identity differed from that of Christians who went before us and from those who now come after us precisely in this, that we were so sure that the Church and the world were compatible and complementary. We had resolved the doubts our elders felt about the inherent goodness and godliness of history and technology, the secular. But of equal importance, we were also sure about the Church. It was of God. Soiled and imperfect as it was, the Spirit was certainly there; slumbering perhaps or enchained, but there nonetheless, and waiting only to be resuscitated. Dry bones, to be sure, but unquestionably "His" bones.

This was our identity then, to bring together these two worlds in both of which we had found the truth. To convince that Church that the world out there was not an enemy, that He was there, too; that, going out, we would not only find ourselves at home, but also helped. To convince the world that we came as genuine friends with things it needed: symbols, insight, and, for its just causes, perhaps even recruits.

But that was an identity for yesterday. Now all that has

changed. Once again our identity as Christians has become a problem. But unlike the previous period, we now feel that we are citizens of no land and aliens in all places that we reside. Indeed, the very terms of the discussion have changed. "Church" no longer names the walls within which we feel at home, and "world" has crumbled into a bewildering congeries of shapes and forms, some hideous, some beguiling, which awaken in us desires, dreams, and doubts that we thought were long since buried or beaten.

To fully analyze the impact on our former sense of identity of the ecclesiastical as well as the political and cultural upheavals of the last few years is beyond the scope of what we can undertake in this paper and at this time. But if we take the title of our inquiry at face value and accept the fact that our identity is in some way Christian, perhaps we can learn something for the present from earlier cultural convulsions, when barbarians confronted Greeks and Romans and Christians were something in between.

There are three different conceptions of Christian identity that emerge for our consideration once we begin to conceive of the present age as analogous to the period of barbarism. The first, or more conservative, view most likely comes in those reactive moments when we are most conscious of the moral and cultural chaos that assaults our eyes and ears in so many different ways today. In moments like these we are apt to conceive of ourselves as defenders of a beleaguered and dying civilization and see ourselves resembling those early Christians who, while they were still cautiously forming their own first interpenetration between Church and culture in classical times, found themselves surrounded by barbarians who did not understand the rules of the game. In a similar way we also have recently seen the questions change before our answers were complete. Drugs, Marx, bombs, marathon encounters, and four-letter words

—these and their panoply tell the story of the last five years in America. Today forces seethe around and inside us calling into question the cultural and political values of ordered change and emotional restraint that we perceived to be so much a part of our first Church-world identity.

But in our less reactive moments, it becomes clear that simply to equate the forces at present challenging Western industrial culture with a destructive and alien barbarism is grossly misleading. For one thing, the first barbarians were persons from foreign or distant territories. Their culture had already been formed without influence from the culture which they challenged and absorbed. But in this geographic and uninfluenced understanding of the term, the latter-day "barbarism" is not an alien force at all. Unlike the former, the modern barbarism comes not from the outside, but from within the culture—from within our universities, our own homes, and even, it must be said, from within the sealed-up caverns of our own bodies and minds. The revolt against what in the argument is called "Western culture" arises from and makes use of the very forces and institutions it seeks to overturn. Those who burn, also pray; who spit, sing; who curse, read; who revel, meditate; and all of us, if we be honest, feel such contradictions stirring inside ourselves. Furthermore, the present-day challenging forces are often the creations of our own hands. The technology whose godliness we so recently celebrated, we now see has inundated us with unordered (i.e., uncivilized) masses of things—of images, of products, of data, and yes, even of people.

But if it will not do simply to equate today's challenges with a barbarism alien to our culture, neither can we simply suppose that, whatever their potential destructiveness, they are inherently or even primarily regressive. To accept such a view is to continue unthinkingly the assumption about the development of Western culture that was already implied in the notion of bridge-builder. At least for so many of us, reaching out to the secular as being of God implicitly assumed a notion of present-day Western civilization as the high point in a series of developmental stages that had as their essential purpose the present development of Western industrial man. In such a view of gradual and directional development, it was assumed that although there were certainly untold numbers of stages still to be reached, we were at the present time pretty much where we were meant to be. Numerous battles had been fought to get there—innocents killed, compromises made, excesses committed—but they were all necessary, more or less, in the development of our civilization and specifically, of its most developed form, the American civilization.

As Christians committed to a bridge-building role between the Church and the world at this juncture, it was our job to take the liberal, developmental, procedural, dispassionate world pretty much as it was and lead it, by Christian spiritual insight, further on its march to the noosphere, that Teilhardian goal toward which, we had now come to perceive, it had in fact been heading all along. Certainly we reserved our right to criticize, and indeed, we perceived our contributions often to lie precisely in a critical or prophetic recall of the society to its own best traditions. But all this was assumed to take place within the framework of that already developed world and in the most enlightened part of the society's formulation of it.

The challenging forces today will not let us continue to play that role, however. In the name of Christian identity itself, voices call on us to take a very different and what can only be called a radical stand toward that very development we once sought to join as well as aid. Daniel Berrigan, for instance, tells us that the present political crisis is so deep and great that "all solutions based on the sanity and health and recoverability of current structures are quickly proven wrong, untimely, unmanageable, bureaucratically infected; the same old kettle of fish, stinking worse than ever in the boiling juice of change." [1] In the name of Christian identity, he tells us that we must "awaken to the facts of life those Americans who continue to grasp at the straws of this or that political promise; and so put off, day after day, year after year, the saving act of resistance, allow innocent men to be imprisoned, guiltless men to be kicked out of America, good men to die." [2]

There are also other critiques which go deeper into the fabric of the culture than does Berrigan's questioning of political institutions. Ray Mungo says of the white heterosexual American male, "he marches around in a getup which everyone else has to laugh at; freaks, spades, chicks, little children, old coots, ladies, madmen, poets, students, and all the apocalyptic sensibilities of the street, all the 'horses of the stern moon' find his shirt and tie and polished shoes unbearably funny, here is a cat trying to pretend something big isn't happening, trying to keep on at business as usual, Clearly he ain't going to make it." [3] Hung up on competition, success, inhibitions, and shame, the only answer for such a man is to throw off all these appurtenances of cultural molding and be his true self. "Whatever you think you are, you are," Mungo says. He tells us, "My program is to go around telling people they're great whenever I can: charming ineffectual flower-child philosophy, you may freely accuse, but since I *believe* it, it's perfect. . . . You're great, you're Christ and Buddha. . . . You're limitless and divine, and your energy can never be destroyed." [4]

It is possible to see a whole new role for Christians emerging in both of these views. Whatever qualification one may be inclined to put on them, it is impossible to listen to these and similar visions and not sense that a very different concept of Christian identity is possible today, and that the Christian as outsider rather than as bridge-builder might be the more ap-

propriate identity for our relation to what we used to call the
modern world.

Daniel P. Moynihan, making use of Anthony Froude's *Origen
and Celsus,* early noted the similarity to today's cultural upheavals in the confrontation between early Christianity and
established civilization, in which the Christians were the barbarians and not the defenders of the established order. He writes,

Who are these outrageous young people? I suggest to you
they are Christians arrived on the scene of Second Century
Rome. . . . "Into the midst of this strange scene of imposture,
profligacy, enthusiasm and craving for light," Froude continues,
"Christianity emerged out of Palestine with its message of lofty
humility."

Who were these Christians? They were first of all outrageous.
They were "bad citizens, refusing public employment and avoiding service in the army; and while . . . they claimed toleration
for their own creed, they had no toleration for others; every
god but their own they openly called a devil. . . ." They had no
temples, no altars, no images, and boasted just that. "Fathers
and tutors, they say, are mad or blind, unable to understand or
do any good thing, given over to vain imaginations. The weavers
and cobblers only are wise, they have the secret of life, they
only can show the way to peace and happiness." Of learning
they had little and cared less. Nor had they any great interest
in respectable people who observed the rules of society and
tried to keep it running; they cared only for the outcast and
miserable. To be a sinner, they seemed to say, was the one sure
way to be saved. They were altogether of a seditious and revolutionary character. . . .

Can there be any mistaking that the New Left speaks to the
rational, tolerant, reasonable society of the present with the
same irrationality, intolerance, and unreasonableness, but possibly also the same truth with which the absurd Christians spoke
to Imperial Rome? [5]

It is easy to recognize the Berrigans and the Mungos in this characterization of early Christianity. Of course, those who are revealing the skeletons locked in the closet by our form of civilized development are by no means mainly Christians. The point at issue, however, is whether Christian identity today means identifying with them in their judgment of ours as a totally discredited civilization. If we are to accept this view, Christian and barbarian identity, instead of being opposite identities as we might first have thought, become one and the same in relation to established civilization.

There is, however, a third form of identity which emerges from the Christian-barbarian parallel. Historically, we know that Christians and barbarians shared another identity than that of critic and outsider. Walter Ong reminds us that if Christians stood with the barbarians in relation to Greek and Roman culture, they were nevertheless the ones who made possible "the assimilation of barbarian by Greek and of Greek by barbarian." [6] It is necessary to consider whether in the cultural convulsions we have been looking at as signaling the emergence of a new barbarism, this other form of barbarian-Christian identity is also operative.

It is a commonplace of popular history to cite the way in which the Christian Church, first in the Greek church fathers and then in the Western monasteries, gave a new lease on life to the philosophical legacy of what in the West at least was a dying culture. Subsequently, often in only the barest rudiments, they also brought civilized learning and order to the newly converted barbarous people who had overrun the disintegrating empire.

To suggest anything like an analogous role for Christians in today's milieu requires, first, that we recall our earlier qualification on any use of the term "the new barbarism." We are *all* uncivilized today—the barbarians are from within, dialectical offspring of the repressed ghosts of established culture's triumph.

There are no existing aristocrats of the new culture already in possession of the goal. As Margaret Mead says of relations between the young and the old today, we are all immigrants in the land of tomorrow.

But if there is in no one's possession any previously validated cultural legacy to be passed on to the new barbarians, it does not follow that a return to pietist asceticism or apocalyptic denunciation, given their inestimable values in keeping our eyes open, is the only contribution the Christian can or should make in the current convulsions. Rather than looking on the bridge-building experience of recent years as part of the cultural baggage to be jettisoned in the uncovering of one's primitive true self, it is possible that what we have learned in that experience can help constitute a practical wisdom, if not a saving gospel, for living faithfully in this world, and particularly in the university, today.

As religious men, the most important dimension of our recent existence has been the experience of God present in his absence. We have seen his traces in the sand, impelling us to carry on while the conviction grew that we were not meant to see him face to face. There have been individuals and people struggling to take control of their lives, and in their very awakening we have recognized the spirit of God struggling to be free. We have experienced historical events as meaningful, leading from one to another not as toward some final perfect goal, but as resulting from what came before and in what came later in ways not seen in advance. Black university students, ostensibly in revolt against a whole society's oppression, discovering the rhetorical and organizational skills of leadership that in a saner day will make them welcome leaders over all the people. White radical students, mentally terrorized by bureaucratic Leviathan, uncovering in their surges its papier-mâché façade and their own freedom to skirt its puppetlike responses. No new Jerusalem here, no promised land of springtime freshness. But in the always surprising manifestations of human strength and resilience, there arises a conviction that we are not just wandering in circles in the desert, but that where we have been was to lead us to where we are now; that where we are now is *meant* to lead to some other place; that the risk of action is always a response to a true call—to the presence of His being.

In responding again and again to that indicated presence we have come to recognize in Jesus the model for facing uncertainty and risk, trusting the *signs* of the Father's presence and then daring to act. Responding to that call we have found ourselves in the struggle for justice experiencing for ourselves the kinds of forces with whom He felt himself at war, the powers and the dominions. We came to see how evil possesses people in a way that overrides their conscious choice and decision, that racism or cultural imperialism, for example, operate irrespective of conscious choice and can only be counteracted by another kind of collective consciousness, by definition a reality not existing with full clarity or even awareness in any given individual. In this experience we began to discover the social function, as distinct from their analytic or explanatory one, of intellectual conceptions and formulations. We discovered the previously unrealized connection between idealism, idolatry, and ideology: that our minds in forming a conception of what society *ought* to be form also a reality which is our hold for the present on that future ideal and as such, i.e., as a mental conception of what ought to be, becomes a given, an "idol" which must be defended, handed down, preserved, and protected as unassailable and unquestioned.

In this new critical awareness of the ideological function of our concepts we began to go beyond the values of liberal, rational society: of individual choice, decision, action. We began to discover the realities of tribe and peoplehood, and politically, the need to think in terms of all the people, the whole, at each moment and not only as some final or future goal in which present injustice and oversight will be righted. In this awareness we came to distinguish the institutions of a people from its inherent spirit. In this way we came, almost simultaneously, to gain a new sense of identity with our rational heritage as Americans and our religious heritage, particularly as Catholic Christians—the loss of innocence about a presumed superiority or moral uniqueness, but also a sense of continuity with parts of our peoplehood previously excluded or downplayed in the more recent ideology of progress and development.

For Catholic Christians in particular there was a renewed sense of identity in the two centuries of protest against what was always called "the modern world": a new appreciation for the uncanny, unreasoned perceptions by apparent reactionaries of Faustian demons in revolutions, political and industrial, that promised to create a very heaven; a new respect for an intuitive recognition of false gods in the images by which bohemian prophets expressed their desperate desire for the infinite. From all of this has come gratitude for a sense of continuity in the present confusion and awareness that the liberal, industrialized cornucopia was not really a celebrated takeoff point for future glories (nor, of course, if it must be said, a cancer to be excised in a return to primitive health), but only a further stage in the struggle for the soul of modern man. The last centuries are now seen not as a march toward progress, but as characterized by the emergence of Leviathan as well as by some of the forces—conscience, choice, freedom—necessary to check it. The current time is seen not as a "now" without parallel in remembered history, but as another moment in that struggle, now come with a vengeance to America's shores, to humanize (i.e., make just) the organized creations required for man's growth and survival.

If there are elements of a practical wisdom contained in this experience for mediating between the old and the new culture, they will of course be relevant to all aspects of society and to many different vocations or roles in it. Reflection upon the relation of this practical wisdom to these different roles is an urgent task for today's Christian. The area in which I feel competent to carry on that reflection is that of the Christian intellectual and, more specifically, the Christian academic. I believe that these elements of a new Christian identity have a particular relevance to the university at this time, both because of the university's origins and deepest impulses and because of the way in which the problems peculiar to the age have expressed themselves there.

It is important to recall first that universities are offspring of monasteries, and monasteries were the center of learning and discipline from which the first barbarism in Western civilization was transcended and civilized. Universities can fulfill their unique role for these times by understanding their present functions in the light of these ancient origins, and it is here that Christians, as particularly sensitive to these origins, and embodying the practical wisdom we have just described, could play an important part.

The first requisite for the university in these times is a healthy respect for the function of service. Like universities whose ideal is the pursuit of truth for its own sake, so monasteries were committed to a function beyond pragmatic measurement, the praise and glory of God. It is possible to say, as many did, that the monasteries were distracted from their essential purpose of contemplating God because former nomads were taught farming within the shadow of their walls. But who today would assert that there was at that time some other better choice facing those men who, in addition to their strong sense of contemplation, felt their neighbors' nakedness with an equal intensity?

This same coming to terms with human need is required of

the university today. In its individual students and surrounding society the university is confronted literally with hordes of persons in need of civilization. We see young undergraduates everywhere seeking to understand the mysteries of their own dreams and desires, turning in desperation to shamans and charlatans, ignored by those who judge them not yet "prepared" for the disciplined discourse about these questions they feel in their guts. Institutions and agencies of higher learning, because they were created in periods of more ordered change, are still governed by the liberal ideology that believes the whole is best served by concentration now on its strongest, best-"developed" parts. Thus only those undergraduates tend to be given special attention who show promise of becoming academic professionals, and questions that bridge the disciplines still find little place or recognition.

William Arrowsmith, himself a scholar of classical literature and one of the most important writers on the contemporary university crisis, points out how the changing cultural scene requires a new and different definition of the university and the individual scholar's role.[7] He declares that the single most determinative factor for life in the university today should be the fact that "in modern times almost the whole job of culture has been dropped on the universities." Such a situation requires a change in the university's traditional ideal, the contemplative-based, pursuit of truth for its own sake. Purists may regret the new burdens placed on the university and consider it an unfortunate development, but Arrowsmith insists that we must not make any mistake about the fact. "Because of the torpor and indecisiveness of the churches, the erosion of communities and family life, the only potentially significant moral and cultural force remaining," he says, "is found in the universities and the colleges."

In the light of this fact, the first priority facing universities today is the extension of this moral and cultural force to the unformed undergraduates. No longer can the university, particularly in its college, relegate the civilizing of its youngest members to their picking up crumbs from specialists' tables. The university and its scholars must begin to give the same kind of systematic attention to the moral and philosophic problems of its young that it has long given to the professional problems of its colleagues and more recently given to the military and social policies of its government.

It will be objected that there is no hard knowledge here, that in such activity scholars are amateurs with no special competence. But most certainly there were no experts on "how to civilize" to be found in the early monasteries either. There was also no general assumption present that a certain stage of cultural and scientific development had been reached, the advancement of which was alone worthy of its members. Popularization, furthermore, was not yet a dirty word. There were present, however, dedicated men aware of new people in new situations in need of what was known from the past, not so much as ready-made answers for the pressing problems of the day, but as useful components in the process of merging man's reason with the complexities of life's survival and development.

Arrowsmith heartily agrees with the proposition that education, of the college young as well as of the graduate professionals, is the proper focus of the university's life. He insists, however, that educating in the sense in which we have just discussed it—the shaping of moral and personal development—means that those who would presume to educate "must be able to command the moral respect, and to enlist the moral energies, of those they are presumably educating. They cannot educate on any other terms." [8]

One can argue that it is precisely the inability to speak with this moral authority on the part of adults today—whether they

be teachers or parents—that accounts for the crisis in the education and formation of the young that is on everyone's mind.
"Why should I take what you say seriously?" is the unspoken
question behind every student's suspicious or contemptuous gaze
in today's classroom. "Why should I focus attention on your
words, or your opinions, rather than those of Dylan or my
friends when you have left this world in a moral, political, and
ecological shambles?"

The issues raised in this question go very deep, as we have
already indicated in our discussion of Berrigan and Mungo, and
as such are beyond the competence of any given individual or
institution. But Arrowsmith indicates a way in which universities
and their personnel can regain at least some of the moral
authority requisite for influential teaching today. He urges that
the men of learning in the universities intensely devote their
energies to the service of the public interest, enlisting in their
work as apprentices (i.e., as learners) the many students seeking
just such involvement as part of their education. He suggests
that the university serve the public interest by itself creating
and running newspapers, television stations, magazines, schools,
welfare agencies, law and medical clinics, etc., that can serve
as alternative models for governmental and private agencies
which are less able to conceptualize a truly universal or public
good. He argues that the universities drop their aristocratic
prejudices and massively enter the economic market by capitaliz-
ing and maintaining these ventures in education and service.
Such a suggestion has the merit, conceivably, of being not just
of practical worth, but educative as well in introducing into the
public consciousness on a wide scale the example of a corporate
body concerned primarily not with its own growth and profit,
but in fact with the general welfare.

It is not necessary to accept Arrowsmith's suggestions in any
given detail, of course, in order to allow his ideas to free one's

own conception of the university from the blinding effects of the ideology of the pursuit-of-truth-for-its-own-sake. It was the greatness and the glory of the Christian monasteries in the early Dark Ages to recognize that the truth they contemplated and sought was to be found not only in their libraries, cells, and choirs but as incarnated as well in the people and their needs all around them. Such an incarnational concept of truth is essential if the monks in these latter-day monasteries are to go beyond their laboratories and podiums to meet the new barbarism which they, as well as all of us, have created, but in the civilizing of which they have a role that no one else is in a position to play.

The Christian's role in the university today lies not only in assisting his colleagues and institutions to come to this incarnational formulation of the truth they seek, but also to recognize in the new barbarism a challenge to its values and an opportunity for a new and possibly richer cultural flowering. Even to recognize this possibility, however, requires a coming to grips with assumptions about the nature of development and civilization, a reassessment which we have already seen has been the experience of the Christian bridge-builder in our times. If the present stage of Western industrial society, granting its many achievements, can no longer be taken as the highest achieved stage in the present evolution of civilization, the same applies, in the field of learning, to the institutions of the society, i.e., its schools and universities. One no longer assumes, for instance, that the future will accept intact the present relation between knowing and doing, feeling and thinking that governs research and learning, and build its achievements on the present, like one building block upon the other.

There are of course other areas in which the university must be willing to entertain fundamental questions about its whole style of operation and function. It must also be willing to reopen the question of its relation to society and its political institutions. The university might once have assumed that liberal democratic political institutions and its own instrumentality for relating to them, the doctrine of academic freedom, were developmental staging points for the future, building blocks to be taken for granted in the next stages of development. But if, as we have come to see, the apparatus of the modern state, even in its representative democratic form, must now be considered as a continuing opponent, as well as a sometime ally, in the struggle for human growth, the university as "the only significant moral and cultural force remaining" may have to assume a much more critical stance toward public officialdom than the present, laissez-faire doctrine of academic freedom (you leave us to do our thing and we'll refrain from mixing in yours) allows. Why should each university law school not have its own chapter of Nader's Raiders? Or its journalism school its own *I. F. Stone Report*?

We might point out in passing that if the university were to undertake the kind of role implied in these few suggestions, one can without much difficulty foresee a struggle shaping up between university and state for which the earlier struggles of monasteries versus princes could be a most suggestive parallel and a situation in which the role of Christian academic and indeed Christian citizen would take on a whole new meaning.

The relevance of what was said earlier about recent Christian experience in Church and world should be invaluable in assisting universities to see and carry out such a role in society. The sensitivity to the role of ideology in institutions, the ability to distinguish between individual and institutional or collective self-awareness and guilt at the heart of blinding purviews, the identity that comes from perceiving one's self in opposition to a people's institutions and structures while knowing that you are allied to its deepest spirit—in helping to contribute these perspectives to the university the Christian academic will find a most important identity and one that is at once faithful to the needs of his time and to the traditions of his tribe and a helpful model to his brothers wherever in society they live or work.

1. Daniel Berrigan in *The Commonweal,* August 7, 1970, p. 385.

2. *Ibid.,* p. 386.

3. Ray Mungo in *The New Republic,* August 15, 1970, p. 24.

4. *Ibid.*

5. Daniel P. Moynihan in *The American Scholar,* Autumn, 1967, pp. 541–542.

6. Walter Ong, *The Barbarian Within* (New York: Macmillan, 1962), p. 285.

7. William Arrowsmith, "The University of the Public Interest," *The Center Magazine,* May, 1970.

8. *Ibid.*

IV

John Meagher:

"Faith is a charism, given to the Church, the corporate body of the faithful. . . . But it is a crippling error to suppose that it defines Christian identity, for its relationship to Christian identity is not a matter of what a Christian claims to be, but what he aspires to become."

IT would have served Elijah right if the Lord had declined to play his grand-standing game with the priests of Baal. He would have been furious. But he wouldn't have been converted to the opposition. And since the Israelite identity crisis would still have remained unresolved, he would have been driven, like all of us who are deprived of timely fire from heaven, to theologize.

"I think there's a theological task that has to be done," a campus minister remarked earlier this year, in the course of a discussion on the crisis of faith. "It has to do with vision, it has to do with claims the numinous makes on us. We talk about those claims in a variety of ways, and for Christians, the numinous, the claim of the numinous, somehow is related to the life, death, and resurrection of Jesus and the Spirit of God. Now what I understand to be the theological task is trying to make concrete the promise of God in relationship to vision, particularly in terms of the cultural movements that are taking place today and the ones that we happen to be involved in. I'm talking particularly about the 'movement' from my involvement."

In the idiom of the Movement—right on! But although this is a representative description of a central concern in the problem of Christian identity, it is still more intriguing as a representative *embodiment* of the problem. In the first place, note that the ultimate religious form to which the speaker appeals is not specifically Christian, but rather, interreligious: we can speak of the numinous in a variety of ways, the Christian way being only one of them. In the second place, note the gingerly and hesitant manner in which the speaker expresses the encoding of numinous vision into Christian terms: for Christians, the numinous *somehow is related* to Jesus and to the Spirit of God. Not that it is the effulgence of Jesus and the Spirit, or that it is the ultimate meaning of Jesus and the Spirit, or even that it is authentically manifested in Jesus and the Spirit—merely that it is somehow related. In the third place, the necessary theological task is said to be the specification of religious vision "in terms of" current cultural changes, a translation of Numinous Promise into the idiom of the Movement. But in the speaker's emphasis on the importance of grasping more clearly the relationship between numen and seething world, he shows little confidence that it could be much to the point to detour the connection via Christianity. Indeed, if the foundational elements of Christianity are only "somehow related" to the numinous, must one not suspect that it would be equally effective and more efficient to make the connection more directly? And thus the traditional determinants of Christian identity drift toward the margin, while the center is taken up with the convergence of generalized religion and particularized cultural involvement.

This is new territory. Most of Christian tradition, lived out in parochial isolation from serious competitors, has taken for granted that the faith was thoroughly numinous and utterly coextensive with authentic religious life. To speak of the numinous apart from Christianity was to risk being either silly or impious. Protected with a heavy cultural overlay, this notion of its own ultimacy and completeness defined Christian identity for centuries. But no more. Largely through its attempts at sympathetic encounter with other world religions, Christianity has learned clearly that it is one of several on a generally similar quest. We have accordingly learned how to describe, and to some extent even how to experience, the character of an underlying *homo religiosus* whose form is not specifically Christian.

But this phenomenon has been around long enough for us to get used to it. We have known for quite some time that underneath one's Christian understanding lies a more ultimate religious disposition that can be described in general religious idioms in which Christianity participates but which are not in themselves derived from Christianity. The numinous is only one of these more general forms. One may also speak of righteousness; of salvation; of enlightenment; of peace; of purity; of communion; of beatitude. These are movements of spirit that are deeper in us than the Christian gospel. Perforce: for how else would we be able to recognize it as good news? It is ultimately at the level described by these categories that we experience and evaluate religious reality, though the experience itself may have to be of concrete particulars. And therefore the discovery that once may have seemed unsettling turns out to be a part of the good news itself: for the congruity of Christianity with the native religious dispositions of man is the indispensable condition for its capacity to bless and perfect our humanity, one of the marks of its authenticity and one of the sources of its power. The same may also be said of other religions, which naturally share Christianity's tendency to develop toward the fulfillment of *homo religiosus*. At this level of inquiry, the claims of competing religions cannot be settled; there is no technique for surveying their peculiarities and differences from one another that can demonstrate the conclusive humanistic superiority of one religion's endowments. Christianity does not monopolize good news, and does not have exclusive access to the depths of *homo religiosus*. It would be unreasonable to require or expect otherwise. For the authentication of Christian identity at that level —which is not the only one, and not necessarily the most important—it is quite enough if the ultimate religious forms find their satisfaction and adequate expression in the stuff of Christianity. That the two strata are not absolutely indistinguishable does not matter.

Or rather, *need* not matter. It still often does, for it has been discouraging for the Christian tradition to awaken from its dream of a definitive apologetics into the harsher light of modern times. The phrase "somehow related to" is a characteristic symptom of a general modern unsettlement of Christian identity, reflecting a loss of confidence both in the credibility of Christianity and in its adequacy as a vehicle of the ideal development of humanity. Sobered by the discoveries of biblical scholarship, chastened by the criticism of analytical philosophy, bruised by physical science, social science, and comparative religion, disappointed by the behavior of the churches, and humbled by the disaffection and hostility of a largely post-Christian environment, the faith of the campus Christian might understandably be expressed in terms that are cautious and apologetically vague. Even more so the most engaged and active of campus Christians, for the movements in which they are involved often bring them into collision with the churches and into collusion with their avowed enemies. To engage in these movements deeply and faithfully entails the development of one's religiously foundational self-understanding, one's sense of the numinous or of righteousness or whatever, in terms of experiences whose coherence with the preoccupations of Christian tradition are sometimes a bit obscure. Hence the urgency felt about translating the Christian promise into the terms of such experience, to make Christianity belong more clearly to the convergence of reverence and revolution, where a new religion sometimes seems to be arising. And thus also, in the meantime, the nagging doubts: Is there any point in trying to be faithful to a Christianity that is both shaky in its public credit and removed from where the action is? Beyond these misgivings, the campus minister must add a still more awkward dilemma: Under such impossible circumstances, can it be either honest or credible (let alone both!) to come on as an Official Christian? The reality of Christian identity on the contemporary campus stands precariously and confusedly between two worlds, one evidently expiring and the other not yet quite born, apparently burdened with the task of being faithful to two masters—and having it on the best possible authority what *that* leads to.

There are several ways of dealing with this identity crisis. One may ignore it by burrowing snugly into some otherworldly version of earlier Christian identity and let the rest of the world go by: the Spiritual Retreat. Or one may acknowledge the changing times just enough to appropriate from the Movement materials for the ornamentation of an otherwise unadjusted stance: new patches on old garments. On the other hand, one may give over the primary allegiance to the other master. On that side of the boundary lie the Post-Christian Leap, a frankly secularized stance which incorporates only as much of the old faith as has sunk through cultural fallout into our bones, and the Christianity of As It Were, which like the former is based on a thought- and language-system of a basically secularist character, but which adds a seasoning of remembered Christian symbols (though it is not always clear whether this is natural or artificial flavoring).

Each of these ways actually has its own integrity as a manner of dealing with the identity crisis, enough so that each deserves a hearing during the quasi-political process by which Christian theology must sort itself out. But alone, none of them will quite do as a way of defining Christian identity in our time.

The first two, Spiritual Retreat and New Patches, make the ancient and discouragingly persistent mistake of presuming that Christian identity has already been thoroughly defined, and that the abiding Spirit has nothing of importance to teach through the news of our time—an assumption which, besides being intrinsically implausible, is hardly the lesson to be derived by studying the behavioral history of the Church. We know it is not so, by the same means by which we respond to the gospel: in the deepest reaches of our reverence, we know good news when we hear it and can recognize the taste of good fruit. As we move within the worlds of today's campus, we know that our Christianity is being taught truths which should belong to it, as well as being reminded of others about which it has been negligent, even if the teaching is under auspices that are far from being explicitly Christian. But not much polemic needs to be spent on reaction against the challengingly new: such a stance is so generally uncongenial to the current campus temperament that it appears to be virtually self-invalidating.

The second pair have a much stronger hold on campus thought, however, and need a bit more attending to. They are attractive in their honesty, responding as they do to various degrees of crisis experienced along the axis of belief; and they are attractive in their modernity, since they are equally responsive to the urgency with which the best instincts of our time regard the axis of relevance. The crisis of Christian identity on today's campus is essentially a crisis of belief and crisis of relevance, and it is on those terms that it must be dealt with.

Difficulties have been arising along the axis of belief for a long time. Not for generations has the Christian world been entirely confident of the truth of traditional Christian identity, formed in the image of Christ the living and coming Lord. The symptoms of disintegration were quiet at first, confined largely to the intricate special interpretations and mental reservations with which Christians addressed themselves to the content of the Church's belief, and a tendency to proclaim only the more modest promises of the gospel. Then came a more direct critical attack, from within the Church, on those portions of traditional belief that were most difficult to reconcile with twentieth-century knowledge and habits of mind. Having found some elements too dependent on discredited prescientific modes of thought (e.g., heaven-in-the-sky, hell-down-below), and others too strongly in league with assumptions that modern intelligence is reluctant to share (e.g., those surrounding the miraculous and the demonic), some of the most able thinkers of the Church set about the task of demythologizing. But what began as an attempt to purge Christianity of false mythical elements tended finally to become a radical reinterpretation. Having properly condemned beliefs that were no longer fit for human habitation, the demythologizing movement went on to condemn others that merely fell below a certain standard of skeptical intellectual comfort. Christians were accordingly encouraged to surrender their notions of the divinity of Jesus, his physical resurrection, the Kingdom to come. Now, in the wake of this movement, comes a vast softening of conviction in such things, manifested by a more public and general symptom: a form of religious discourse and religious practice detached from Christian particulars and concretely defined in ways that all modern minds might accept—only "somehow related" to the traditional doctrinal and liturgical foundations of Christianity.

It is not difficult to understand how modern sensibilities might find themselves more at ease with this Christianity of As It Were. It solves the tension of belief. An identity thus formed wears more comfortably, fits closer to the skin. There is something obviously right about its honesty, and something apparently efficient in the directness of its appeal to the general forms of *homo religiosus*. These criteria have their own limitations, of course: honest and comfortable religion (as critics of the Church know well) can be deceptive and can relax the very tensions on which significant growth depends—and it is still not clear that the direct formation of *homo religiosus* through generalized religion is necessarily more effective than raising *homo sapiens* with symbolic logic as his mother tongue. But the real point of objection lies elsewhere: it is that nothing so unnecessarily discontinuous with the Christian past can provide an adequate solution to the problem of *Christian* identity. There are indeed new forms of religious integrity available on the other side of the Post-Christian Leap, but it is not appropriate to call them unqualifiedly Christian.

If circumstances require Christian identity to serve two masters in order to be faithful, there is still one other way offered by our time, standing between the two pairs discussed above and far less likely to self-destruct as an identity that is both contemporary and Christian. This is the Christianity of At Least: an attempt to negotiate an honorable compromise by discerning in the self-understanding of modern consciousness structures of meaning that are genuinely cognate (though not identical) with the contents of traditional Christian belief—locating Christian identity in the terrain in which the claims of both masters overlap. This form of demythologizing, not nearly as radical as the other, is attractive enough to have won wide acceptance as a way of preserving both Christianity and modernity: from it have come a fleet of new experimental creeds, scaled down to the level of general reservations and defining Christian faith in terms of those features of traditional Christianity which the contemporary Christian may *at least* believe.

Taken by itself, however, this route is not quite satisfactory. Although it attempts to be faithful to both the Christian tradition and the modern mind, it really compromises both. To propose diminished belief as the equivalent to traditional belief, even if the diminution is only partial, is to beg the question and confuse the issue. No good purpose is served by trying to pretend that the earlier Christian Church did not believe what it thought it believed, nor by trying to pretend that we mean the same things if in fact we don't. And we are not in a position to claim confidently that it does not matter: it has always mattered in the past and has left an impress on the Christian tradition which no one seeking Christian identity can decisively discredit or properly ignore. So where can we go from here?

The basic thrust of these attempted solutions seems to me quite right. Some form of demythologizing is unavoidable, especially for the Christianity of the campus, where the tension

of belief is most acute. But what is wrong with these attempts
is that they mislocate the myth. They strike at the *content* of
Christian belief, when what is called for is, rather, a demythologizing of *form*—that is, not *what* beliefs are held, but rather
how they are held.

The really troublesome myth is the supposition that all
Christians relate to the Church's belief with a faith that brings
total personal conviction. Like all myths, this has its element of
truth: from the beginning, there have undoubtedly always been
such believers, whose wholeness of faith would not have left
room for the least knife-edge of irony or doubt. They were, and
remain, the paradigmatic cases of Christian faith. But they are
paradigmatic in the sense that they represent the ideal limit:
this is the condition of faith to which the Christian is called to
aspire. Its relationship to Christian identity is not that it defines what a Christian claims to *be,* but rather what he may
become. The proper way of demythologizing belief is to recognize that the hope of becoming is an authentic and characteristic Christian disposition.

The problem of sin taught the Church at an early stage the
difference between what the Christian claims to be and what he
hopes to become. But with respect to the question of belief, a
combination of ecclesiastical discipline and strong cultural
complicity have obscured the same distinction, fostering a myth
of faith which has endured remarkably long—but with which
the Church can no longer live. A hope that is strong, un-
challenged, and firmly supported by one's community may
easily be mistaken for full belief: and so it was in the case
of the ordinary Christian in earlier times. It is not hard to see
how the myth persisted. But in the world in which the Church
now lives, the previously obscured distinction is forced upon
us. It is therefore not a question of a loss of faith, but merely
a more accurate relocation of its boundaries now that cultural

circumstances require us to take greater intellectual responsibility for the sources and degrees of our conviction. To join oneself in hope and love to the belief of the Christian Church is, and has always been, to participate authentically in Christian faith.

In the inner wellsprings of religious life, one begins with the hope of religious fulfillment and the love of its Bestower. If one finds in Christianity a fruitful ground for the nourishment and development of this hope and love, one has already made an implicit act of faith by which one begins to participate in the Church. If at this stage one still does not or cannot yet believe confidently everything the Church proposes to him as the content of its formal faith, one may nevertheless love it enough to entertain it with reverent seriousness, and hope that an authentic faith may be fostered by sharing in Christian life. In earlier times, this was the condition of the catechumen during his preparation for entry into the Church; circumstances strongly discouraged both the discovery and the admission that it is also, when belief is subjected to more rigorous scrutiny, the condition of the ordinary Christian, even if it is not that of the perfected Christian. We have since made both the discovery and the admission—along with the realization that Christian identity is not undermined by difference between the faith of the Church and the faith of its members.

For belief is not given fully to each member of the Church. Faith is a charism, given to the Church, the corporate body of the faithful, and is the objective correlative of the communal experience of belief as lived out by the Church in history. This is what the Creed symbolically expresses in its enactment of the belief of the corporate body, and the first-person-singular of the Creed would accordingly be more appropriately understood as that of the Church than that of the individuals who compose it. The latter may also believe individually what the Creed formulates for corporate understanding, but the Church has always understood such a faith as a special gift. It is not ours for the asking, and can hardly be supposed to be definitive of authentic Christian identity. It describes the paradigmatic case, the accumulated tradition of belief toward which the Christian is invited to aspire. But in the meantime, until such aspiration is fulfilled, faith need not be complete to be authentically Christian. Through hope and love, the identity of the Christian may transcend the limits of his belief, participate in the faith of the Church, and become unmythically and unpretendingly real.

Such a mode of Christian identity seems to me both honest and credible. But not, for all that, complete. Faith is not all that Christianity is, and surely not all that it is supposed to be. It claims to be the Way and the Life as well as the Truth.

Here arise more collisions between Christian identity and the contemporary campus ethos, and the problems thus raised along the axis of relevance are often even more acute than the problem of belief. The Church promises, and even lays claim to, a more abundant life. Is such a claim credible when tested for vitality against the quickened pulse of modern ideals? Not obviously, it seems. In the vital center of contemporary campus life, one finds persistently a deep misgiving: What has the Christian heritage to do with *now,* with understanding and action in the face of the needs and urgencies of our time? What has Christianity to do with what we find ourselves and our world becoming? Neither Spiritual Retreat nor New Patches can provide an answer: these are merely ways of avoiding the most radical form of the question and retreating from the forms of life through which an answer might be achieved. Again, the stronger inclinations are toward a harsher judgment on Christianity. Surveyed from the rather impatient perspective of leading campus movements, it looks neither especially convincing in the present nor especially promising for the future. Despite the fact that Christianity has long dreamed of peace and of radical justice and of human brotherhood, it has not shown much capacity to generate from its own private heritage the solutions now urgently needed—and has even been disappointingly sluggish in its response to the problems. Thus self-betrayed, it does not obviously merit anything better than the nostalgic concessions of As It Were or the bolder rejection of the Post-Christian Leap.

There is no dodging the accusation. Individual leaders have proved the vitality and relevance of their Christianity to the Movement; but in general, the underdevelopment of the Christian heritage, and of the contemporary Christian Church, is nowhere more glaringly evident than in precisely those areas with which the best spirits of today's campus culture are especially preoccupied. In the light of what they know and want, the Church seems embarrassingly naïve and negligent about the character and needs of human societies and of life in this new time—so scandalously short of revolutionary cash value that if the trial of relevance is conducted brusquely and exclusively according to these perceptions, the verdict is predictable. It only remains to be decided whether the sentence imposed shall be death, life imprisonment in marginal acts of piety, or imposed bankruptcy.

But if the trial of relevance appeals *exclusively* to these considerations, it is a rigged trial, and embodies an unreal and desperate demand—reminiscent of the late inquiry about what it means to be a Christian physicist. It is, in fact, the most up-to-date and seductive version of that form of Pharisaism which righteously condemns any movement that hobnobs too intimately with unfashionable kinds of sinners. It is to be granted that Christianity has been too preoccupied with restricted ways of being the Truth, and that it has been sadly negligent about preserving and developing its own self-understanding as Way and

Life. It has a great deal to learn and to remember. But such a realization is neither scandalous nor novel. The incompleteness and insufficiency of the Church are among the permanent facts of life and of history, but they are not in themselves proof of either obsolescence or senility. There is a limit to what may legitimately be asked, and another to what may reasonably be expected. It may be appropriate to prod the universities into greater involvement in pressing contemporary problems, but it is not helpful to pretend that it is within their competence to eliminate suffering. The Church deserves a similar sanity from its disappointed critics, and a little patience.

It also deserves a less narrow standard of judgment, and a more impartial judge. If the trial is to be fair, then one must hear all the claims on both sides. It must be remembered that the question of relevance may cut two ways. It is not only a matter of what Christianity can deliver to the concerns that most preoccupy me (and this, when fairly examined, turns out to be quite a bit), but also whether I have permitted the pattern of my concerns to be sufficiently relevant to the preoccupations of Christianity. If I refuse to deal seriously with the latter kind of relevance, there is no fair and balanced way for me to come to terms with the problem of Christian identity. Nearly two thousand years of Christian experience have been lived out, all of it modern in its own day. Its value and importance should be evident to anyone who bothers to learn about it, and the basic style of Christian identity which carried and preserved that experience therefore has a claim to make. It deserves freedom from being eviscerated by the scalpel of a benevolent but undiscriminating urgency, or from being put away as a result of a mistaken diagnosis. Not that it offers a legitimate refuge from the truth of our times, or invites us to evade the task of redefinition. Campus Christianity cannot leave the old priorities untouched, or survive exclusively on an identity which, like all identities, is partially obsolete. It must be creative in order to be faithful. But both its creativity and its fidelity are too important and holy not to be taken with the utmost seriousness. And therefore, when we anticipate with properly hopeful excitement that a new Christian identity will be forged through the response of campus Christianity to the movements of our time, let us not, in our enthusiasm, forget that the word *forged* can carry two quite different senses.

We stand between two worlds, I remarked a while back, one not yet quite born and the other apparently expiring. How does such a world die? It dies the way a wisdom dies: by being abandoned.

Christianity was never easy, and rarely obvious. I expect that most Christians, at one time or another, have wished enviously that theirs could be the hard way of Paul, driven relentlessly by the demands of the gospel but fully possessed by it: "I am not ashamed of the gospel of Christ, for it is the power of God unto salvation to every one that believeth." That might be easier to deal with than the way it usually is: the difficult business of opting continually to sustain the demands of a Christian identity that has not yet transfigured us. But we must start from where we are. Our Christianity has, after all, only been offered, not imposed. Much of it is probably easy enough to shake off if one wishes to do so. It has already been weakened by having been deprived of our courageous dedication to what it demands of our active lives. It can be allowed to die to us if we merely withhold from it the faith, hope, and love on which its remaining power and vitality depend, reducing it to a museum of thinkable but only figurative symbols. But to suppose this inevitable is to misunderstand history; and to suppose that the authority of Christianity is obliged to make itself felt independently of our response to it is to misunderstand not only religion but the human condition. We cannot escape responsibility for the formation of the world in which we are to live and find our meaning. We are sentenced to choose. There is no way of avoiding involvement in the life or the death of Christian identity, for neither can take place except through the ways in which we constitute our lives, with it or against it. What can guide our choice?

For an answer, we must return to precisely those canons of judgment by which the crisis of Christian identity was made acute in the first place: belief and relevance. And the inescapable truth is that when I survey what I really believe, I find that it goes beyond the boundaries of generalized religion. It includes not only the authenticity of Jesus as a manifestation of the holy truth, and the congruence of his gospel with what I would ultimately wish to become, but also the revealing importance of the Christian experience as history reports it, the rightness of what the Christian body in its best and most lucid moments has tried to be and to give to the world, the way in which the Church's demanding good news about Christ, the living and coming Lord, echoes in me like a judgment and a calling home. These things do not come to me as the bones of a dead and dying world: they are living data of my present experience for which I must take responsibility. As a way of being faithful to their reality, I choose not to withhold my trust in those whose experience of them is more intimate than mine, or the hope and love which they invite for the Christian claims and promises which my faith can not yet reach. And so also with relevance: not only does my Christian identity deliver to me something valuable in myself, something I have never found a way to receive at any other hands, but when I listen reverently to the testimony of the traditionally Christian modes of consciousness, I find in them a peculiar ability to affirm and encourage what I recognize as life, to perceive the holiness of the new passion for peace and justice and to be at home in it, to value what our time has newly discovered and yet to transcend the provinciality and self-deception of this and of all present moments. I find a perspective that I experience as both fruitful and wise. If these are not important dimensions of relevance, then I cannot think how the term is to be used.

The world of traditional Christianity has not yet expired, and our understanding of Christian identity should continue to sustain its claims and to participate in its demands—for it is not that Christianity has failed, but merely that it has been found too difficult to master. To acknowledge the rights and virtues of its enduring invitation is no impediment to participation in the birth of a new world, and may be a valuable protection against the danger of miscarriage. It would be rather glib and starry-eyed to deny, for instance, that the Movement's courage and energy have sometimes been turned to brutal uses, or that the new mood would be more promising if it participated more in the discipline of a tradition more wise and experienced—and for all that, no less generous—than itself. Not all that is hatched by zeal is holy, and in the occasional friction between Christian principles and campus revolution, it is not always the former that needs shaping up. Neither one nor the other alone, then: for although no man can serve two incompatible masters, we are all required to honor both father and mother.

If Christianity is to stay alive, however, it is not enough for it to protect its tradition. It must develop new tradition, which it will do in living new life. Here again, the Christianity of the campus will be especially important, particularly in the mode which I have described before as the Christianity of At Least.

I suggested earlier that the Christianity of At Least is, when taken by itself, not a satisfactory solution to the problem of modern Christian identity. But the alternative solution which I have tried to outline does not totally exclude At Least: on the contrary, this not only permits it to be validly included within the life of the Church, but virtually requires it. For although the Church itself continues to propose the received paradigm, the condition to which it is hoped that the Christian will attain, we need also to understand Christian identity as lived. Within its horizons are varieties of degrees and ways in which faith has turned to bone and spirit in the lives of aspiring Christians. Their Christian identity is defined ultimately and hopefully in terms of the belief and life of the Church; but it is also defined currently and substantially by what they have thus far come to believe and to live. It is in this way that the compromise embodied in the Christianity of At Least becomes an honorable one: it expresses helpfully and honestly the living (if incomplete) faith of the Christian without confusing it with the ultimate (if unfinished) faith of the Church.

But if the Church listens well to this testimony, it will discover that something new has been added. From her traditional perspective, this is the Christianity of At Least, insofar as it has partially realized the Church's own ideal; it is not the whole of Christian identity. But if the perspective is enlarged to include the growth endemic to living things, this becomes the Christianity of Also: if it does not incorporate and incarnate all that the Church holds dear, it nevertheless absorbs and offers to the life of the Church new possibilities, new priorities, new styles of dedicated life. The Christian identity of Also is both less and more than traditional Christian identity, and is the indispensable way of growth for the living Church. It is in precisely this mode of Christian self-consciousness that the Church experiments and learns—appropriates into its own life discoveries made elsewhere, so that their spirits may be tested and discerned.

This is not a cozy process. The Church has always comprised elements of undiscriminating faddishness, too ready to reroute the life of the Church down some ephemeral dead end, and elements of undiscriminating reaction, too starkly inhospitable to news to bother coming to terms with it even when it is clearly good. But harmony, as the ancients contended, is a function of discord. There is bound to be a lot of the latter as the Church undertakes its current homework, and it must accordingly increase its tolerance, trusting that the truth will prevail—not by fiat or by fad, but by being lived. And of all the life of the Church, the segment that is most importantly relevant to this process right now is probably the Christianity of the campus, where the new news is being most vividly and demandingly proclaimed. It is especially through the living out of the identity of the campus Christian that we shall eventually discover what of it belongs to Christ.

And it is likewise only through such a process that the Church can know who and what is the Christ in whom it believes. For at the root of the Church's life lies the conviction that itself, the Christian body, is the continued manifestation in history of the Lord whose office, meaning, and nature are disclosed in the development of the life and belief of the Church. At the point of its origin stands the Jesus of Faith, in whose authenticity every Christian, no matter how small his endowment of faith, may readily believe. This is the Jesus of Faith whom Cleopas acknowledged as a man, a prophet, mighty in work and in word before God and all the people—the one who was publicly manifest and whose credibility was, and is, sufficiently evident through the mere Jonah-sign of his message and his deeds. The Jesus of Faith is the first principle of Christianity. It is in the Jesus of Faith that the Church discovered the second principle, the Christ of History, the Lord who guides his people as himself, shaping their life and their understanding as long as history shall endure.

The Church is forever engaged in the process of understanding the Christ of History through its life as Christ in History, going about his Father's business. Precisely how the Church's encounter with the new world of the campus movements will affect its understanding of itself and the Christ of History remains to be seen. We can know only that such heady new wine is bound to stretch and reform the old skins. That is the way it has always worked. We cannot yet predict what more of the Church's belief will eventually go the way of the apostolic expectation of a first-generation Parousia, nor what may be added through the new spirits, as the Church once learned to repent of her toleration of slavery. Our task is simply to go about this business faithfully, with as much mutual trust as we can summon. Such faithfulness does not require us to repudiate the past in order to participate in the formation of the future, or to suppose that the authenticity of campus Christianity depends upon identifying "the *real* Christianity" with what is palatable to radical secularism, or what is immediately negotiable in action, or even with our own brands of the Christianity of Also. To be faithful must mean both to preserve and to create. In both, one must be generous, and careful, and daring, because there is no trick of theological engineering that can protect our choices from cowardice masquerading as prudence, or from recklessness disguised as Vision. Or even from Movement disguised as Christianity. There will be time for new harmonies to arise out of new discords, as long as we remember that nothing less than the reverent appropriation of Christianity's whole experience, past and present, can provide a sufficient basis for the discernment of spirits.

So when we are told that "He is in the desert" and "He is in the secret chambers," or "He is in the Scriptures" and "He is in the Old Way," we are to believe in the finality of none of these: but we are to attend seriously to all of them, and to those who live them, because this is the way in which Christianity searches for its ultimate identity. What that identity will ultimately be, as belief, or as worship, or as style of life, we cannot know. What her members can no longer hope, the Church can no longer believe; and what her members come to be, the Church will absorb into her life and understanding. But as long as men can continue to believe in the Jesus of Faith, Christianity will endure; and as long as they continue to love and hope in the Christ of History, At Least is not the last word in the definition of Christian identity; and as long as the Church can trust in the guidance of the Christ of History, it must acknowledge the validity of the Christianity of Also as a part of the Way, the Truth, and the Life through which it is led by and toward its hidden Lord. In the meantime, the Christianity of the campus must continue, like the Body of Christ everywhere, to be about its Father's business: no good work need be compromised, no faithful witness need be restrained, and no man need be ashamed of the gospel of Christ.

V

Richard A. Underwood:

"Christian identity on today's campus? It is the resurrection of the body, the new sensibility, the new testament. But there is still no word, no conversation, no hearing from one another. . . . There is singing, dancing, praising: but it remains still at the level of revelry, . . . not a conversation in which the heavenly ones are named."

The Subjunctive Mood: It is easy to state what Christian identity *should* be on today's campus. It should be a catalytic function to facilitate the creation of peace, harmony, understanding, love, compassion, true learning, expanded and deepened awareness. Christian identity should be an enabling presence, transforming today's campus into a halfway house for gentle, sustained, disciplined, and imaginative experimentation for a creative, and not destructive transition from the traumas of adolescence to the new trials of adulthood. Christian identity should be, on today's campus, a way, a truth and a living which transforms violence and unnamable fear and anxiety into creative tension. Christian identity should change abstract, bureaucratic, computerized, impersonal, pedantic, political pedagogy into the living word, which induces receptivity in place of aggression, which educes caring in place of grasping, and which produces both wholeness able to encompass radical change and self-ness instead of isolation.

There are two quite obvious difficulties with this beginning.

The first is: it is easy to state what *should* be the case, but it is profoundly difficult, if not impossible, to say how what should be *could become*. A powerful temptation manifests itself here. That is: leave the question of Christian identity as it stands—in the subjunctive mood—and forget the more difficult problem of how to translate the subjunctive into the indicative. Part of the difficulty here is that nothing new can be said. It seems that everything that could be said has been said. It is evident, then, that saying or writing is no longer enough. But let us suppose that something new *could* be said. Then it would not be understood. Supposing, however, that it could be understood, then it would not be new. So we begin to sense a different mood: the mood of exhaustion and despair. The temptation, then, is to retreat into silence. The power of this temptation is compounded, since it is an alternative so rarely tried. Perhaps—

so far as Christian identity is concerned—the time of silence has come. Then the Christian prolegomena would be *not* "in the beginning was the word," but rather, "in the beginning was the no-word." The trouble with that is—it is still a word!

The second difficulty in beginning with a statement of what Christian identity on today's campus *should be* is that the content of the statement could be subscribed to by other modes of identity. One could, that is, adduce other religious, political, psychological, or ideological positions which would not take exception to the beginning answer offered in the subjunctive mood. We have, for instance, "The Dawning of the Age of Aquarius" (the overture to *Hair: The American Love-Rock Tribal Musical*), in which the appeal is not to Christ as the paradigm of Christian identity. It is, rather, an appeal to the zodiacal process of the stars and the planets. But, is a viable Christian identity going to take exception to the appeal to *love* as that which will "steer the stars" or to "Harmony and Understanding, Sympathy and Trust abounding"? Cannot Christian and astrologist agree on the desirability of these promises becoming present—even though one promissory note is signed *Jupiter and Mars* and the other is signed *Christ*? Jesus himself taught that the fruit of the tree is more important than its name.

We are confronted, then, with two difficulties: on the one hand, simply stating the subjunctive and letting it go at that; on the other hand, seeing that other identities do not cavil at the virtue of Christian identity as stated in the beginning; and seeing too that *both* difficulties tempt one to silence. It is in the area (or the "space/time between") in the *middle* that our question asserts itself most powerfully and insistently.

Breathing Together and Speaking Together: "Christian identity on today's campus" is a question of immense importance, since the cultural context in which psychic identity has been set forth during the past several centuries is that of biblical legend. The problem is that the legend has been taken too seriously. In being taken too seriously it has been taken too literally. In being taken too literally, the reading/saying (the legend) has been killed: the letter kills, but the spirit gives life. The connection between the literalism of the letter which kills and the lifelessness of today's campus scholarship (*not* today's campus *life*) is suggested by Norman O. Brown:

> Protestant literalism is modern scholarship. Parallel to the emphasis on the one true meaning of scripture there was an increase in Luther's interest in grammar and textual criticism; to establish the text, die feste Schrift, a mighty fortress; the authoritative text.[1]

But the text/legend is no longer *author*-itative: it is sensed, experienced, interpreted as written by somebody else, aliens in a strange land; the sense of familiarity has been lost. So Brown also suggests:

> The identification of God's word with scripture, the written or printed word; somewhat to the neglect of the word made flesh. The book is a materialization of the spirit; instead of the living spirit, the worship of a new material idol, the book.
>
> There is also the new hierarchy of scribes, controlling the interpretation, the higher scholarship. . . .[2]

What are we to conclude? Today's campus in America—and throughout the world—has become a microscope through which the malaise of the modern spirit has been magnified for all to see. What else are we to expect? Are not the iniquities of the fathers visited upon the children unto the third and fourth generations? Today's campus is the consummation of a cultural experience which has stressed, both implicitly and explicitly, the ideology of the book and the value of performance. But the campus children have revolted against the book and are seeking the open spaces of the field. The only fields left to them for an opening are those of interior, psychic, and intellectual exploration: there are no seas to run away to, no wild lands await. In short, sublimation of the inner quest no longer seems possible. Reformation, then, now turns inward: the new frontier is the psychic life of a culture which is experienced as sick within, and the fathers, not knowing of their iniquities, are dethroned by the children of today's campus who know no other direction in which to move except the *inner-most*.

Here we experience a bind: culture is to *enliven;* but the legends of our culture, in being taken too seriously, too heavily, are *enervating*. What we are confronted with is a "failure of nerve" transformed into a dearth of spirit—spirit become dear, precious, in a time when all is heavy, fallen, grave, and thus hidden. It is, it seems, a fulfillment of Nietzsche's insight: ". . . when I saw my devil I found him serious, thorough, profound, and solemn: it was the spirit of gravity—through him all things fall." [3] Before this, Nietzsche had written: ". . . of all that is written, I love only what a person hath written with blood, and thou wilt find that blood is spirit." [4]

Part of the problem of today's campus is that the legends— the books, the reading/sayings—have become bloodless, and thus spiritless. Brown cites Emerson's Phi Beta Kappa address:

The Books of an older period will not fit this. Yet hence arises a grave mischief. The sacredness which attaches to the act of creation, the act of thought, is transferred to the record. . . . Instantly the book becomes noxious: the guide is a tyrant . . . I had better never see a book than to be warped by its attraction clean out of my own orbit, and make a satellite instead of a system. The one thing in the world, of value, is the active soul.

Then Brown observes:

> How far the university is from that ideal is the measure of the defeat of our American dream.
> This bondage to books compels us not to see with our own eyes; compels us to see with the eyes of the dead, with dead eyes. . . .[5]

The revolt on today's campus can be traced to those who are seeking a new legend, a new myth, if you will, to replace "the Books of an older period," and thus resurrect the culture which, in the sensibility of the minority on the young side of majority, inculcates death rather than life.

The best possible construction to be put on this revolt [revolt: "to cast off (or change) allegiance; to rise against rulers or constituted authority"] is that it seeks to turn death into life by resurrecting the spirit of the word. What is being sought, and the seeking is the revolt, is the living word of new beginnings. The living word proceeds from the original elements: the earth which nourishes the body speaking, the air expired by the lungs, the water which moistens the lips, the fire of inspiration. The word so spoken, the word of beginnings, gathers these elements together to create a new world. In such speaking is re-creation, experienced by the elders, whose allegiance is to "the Books of an older period" as revolt.

Here we have reached directly the "space/time between" in which the possibility of Christian identity, as a catalytic function, can be creatively present. The "space/time between" is that of a "double lack, a double not": the no-more of the legends that have been killed by the letter, the not-yet of the legend resurrected by the spirit.[6]

What, then, is Christian identity to be in this "space/time between" which we call today's campus? Further, how are we to avoid the fault of saying what ought to be the case of Christian identity without giving some clues as to how it might *become?*

The answer to the first question lies in the response to the second question. What ought to be is already showing itself as becoming. The problem, however, is this: what is showing itself as becoming is showing itself in apparent independence of Christian identity. We are, so to speak, confronted with two unknowns: the unknown of Christian identity and the unknown of today's campus, recognizing that what is at this moment called *today's* campus will soon be *yesterday's* campus. In any event: Christian identity on whatever is or will become today's campus could be seen as functioning like the jar in Wallace Stevens' poem:

> I placed a jar in Tennessee,
> And round it was, upon a hill.
> It made the slovenly wilderness
> Surround that hill.[7]

The image functions so as to recall the opening verses of the first chapter of Genesis:

In the beginning God created the heaven and the earth.
And the earth was without form, and void; and darkness was upon the face of the deep. And the Spirit of God moved upon the face of the waters.
And God said. . . .

The connection is this: in the Genesis legend the first two actions are *breathing* ("the Spirit . . . moved upon the face of the waters") and *speaking* ("and God said . . ."). There is no speech without breath. The Lord God's breath-speech is the jar-ing which transforms the "slovenly wilderness" into *world,* turns it into creation out of chaos. By the same token, then, Christian identity on today's campus becomes a breathing-speaking together; that is, it becomes a bodily gesture [gesture: to bear or carry, to take on oneself, take charge of, to perform or accomplish;[8] also see gesture in relation to *suggest,* which is to speak]. Further: this identity becomes a con-spiracy, a breathing-together, issuing in speech, which creates a new world.

Martin Heidegger quotes the poet Hölderlin:

> Much has man learnt.
> Many of the heavenly ones has he named,
> Since we have been a conversation
> And have been able to hear from one another.

Then Heidegger observes: "We—mankind—are a conversation. The being of men is founded in language. But this only becomes actual in *conversation.*" [9]

Christian identity on today's campus? Breathing-together, hearing from one another, conspiracy/conversation. In the conversation resides the possibility of naming the "heavenly ones." If the heavenly ones remain nameless, then today's campus is not a complete conspiracy/conversation. We hear from one another only if the solitude of our existence is gathered up into *world* which holds us all together. It is a holding together that arises out of conversation which names not only the earthly speakers but also the "heavenly ones."

Heidegger speaks of "the foursome" (*Gevierte*[10]) which "interplays" to bring world into being. The "foursome" are: the earth, the sky, mortals, gods (the "heavenly ones"). Authentic conversation displays all of these in their organic and ontological unity. The image Heidegger employs is that of a pitcher pouring out either wine or water. The water is drawn from the earth, the earth is fed by the rains from the sky. The water may quench a man's thirst; it may be used as a libation for the gods to honor another mortal—one's son, daughter, lover, or friend. The libation, the honoring, is not only a giving of water or wine voicelessly: it is a giving with a speaking—a toasting. Hence in conversation is rooted the possibility of naming the "heavenly ones"; but the naming of the heavenly ones is the completion of conversation.

Christian identity on today's campus is a completion, a "foursome-ing" which transforms chatter into conversation, which transforms cocktail banter into enchantment, an incantation which turns the useful into the present. But here we are confronted with a problem: it has to do with the "space/time between"—the no-more of the legends killed by the letter, the not-yet of the legend resurrected by the spirit. Conversation now is *incomplete* not only because holy names are lacking. It is incomplete because the earth, the body, the blood-spirit, is dried up. It is no longer wet, moist; and because it is heavy and grave it is no longer airy. Hence we have not conversation but chatter, babel. There is also a different dimension to the double lack of the "space/time between" of today's campus: the no-more of the gods, the heavenly ones; and the no-more of the earthly ones, the mortals. The earthly ones *are* only as they converse with each other, hear from one another; but this conversing *becomes* only as the conversation names the gods. In the double-not of the gods and the earthly ones today's campus is not a "foursome," not a world, but limbo.

In this double lack, Christian identity as a catalytic function conspires/converses within the void, the in-betweenness, out of its own history, the tradition of its own conversation and world-creating. What is being proposed is simply this: Christian identity on today's campus, as a conspiracy/conversation, can function as a double presence in the midst of the double lack of the "space/time between." It functions dialectically: in naming the heavenly ones it resurrects the body/text/legend;

in resurrecting the body/text/legend it names the heavenly ones. In doing both it creates conversation, the "foursomeness" of the world.

What remains is an explication of these perhaps seemingly cryptic remarks—the resurrection of the body from the tomb of these remarks. What follows will be nothing new. Now, however, it seems plain that something new is not needed. What is needed is a rediscovery of the old, the archaic, the *arche,* the beginning—so that together we may rebind ourselves in wholesome unity with the original elements. I solicit your help in seeing and saying deeper than I can write. Here is a point at which speaking and writing have something in common: speaking is completed only in the *hearing;* writing is completed only in the *reading.* In this completion is the possibility of world as conversation—we hear from one another.

Resurrection of the Body and "Naming of the Heavenly Ones": We have posited today's campus as a "space/time between," exhibiting in two aspects a double lack, a double not: (1) the no-more of the legends killed by the letter, the not-yet of the legend resurrected by the spirit; (2) the no-more of the "heavenly ones" and the no-more of the "earthly ones"—the mortals. What the second dimension of the double lack is meant to point to is this: the earthly ones, *man the mortal,* has become desiccated, dry, bloodless, spiritless. This may be because of the bread we eat! If we are what we eat, then consider this observation by Alan Watts in "Murder in the Kitchen":

Much may be learned about a civilization from its staple food which, in our case is supposed to be bread. Real bread is a solid and crusty substance with an aroma evoking visions of farm kitchens, flour mills, sacks of wheat, and rolling, waving fields of grain, gold and gentle in the lazy heat of a late summer after-noon. Few Americans have such associations and our bread does not suggest them, being a virtually weightless compound of squishy and porous pith injected with preservatives and allegedly nutritive chemicals. It is not so much white as ideally and per-fectly colorless, and approximates—as nearly as human genius can manage it—to the taste of absolute nothingness. . . .[11]

It would be interesting if the wheat-growing and bread-baking industries would collaborate to produce, under the new tech-nological capabilities, a new bread which would recover the qualities of the old bread. A new "old" bread might then be-come the foursome, a bread in which we could taste, smell, touch, and feel the earth that nourishes, the sun and rain from the sky. With such a bread true sharing with other men, worthy also of a blessing invoking the heavenly ones, would become possible. If we are a conversation, then the possibility of that conversation is the bread and wine we eat and drink together.

In this context we should note that the fundamental phil-osophical question of the past three centuries has been and still is "What is man?" The question "Who am I?" is asked only when the sense of my identity has been lost and when I realize that what I am presently experiencing does not "fit" with what I vaguely remember as who I *was*.

Further, for man to ask the question "Who am I?" is for him to affirm at the same time the death of the heavenly ones. If the gods were still lively, then I would be able to hear from them and know: "I am the one who hears from the heavenly ones." But on the other hand, the "heavenly ones" may disap-pear because I have disappeared. *They* no longer hear from *me*. So they retreat into silence. Man and the heavenly ones can be only insofar as they address each other in conversation. Neither can be unless each hears from the other. The retreat of the heavenly ones, their silence, issues from the ceasing of man's speaking with them. In the ceasing of this speaking man also disappears. Man's body becomes heavy and spiritless; it sinks into the ground and all becomes unconscious. The silence of "the heavenly ones" and the loss of the body: regression which serves neither the heavenly nor the mortal ego. In the meantime forces take over, forces with which man cannot converse; man becomes once again victim and victimized because he no longer knows how to listen and speak. There is a whole catalogue of misery. When the power of conversation is lost then world disappears, the earthly ones disappear, and the heavenly ones disappear. Where world *was* chaos *is* once again, awaiting breathing and speaking anew. In the meantime the chaos manifests its *an-arche*.

One aspect of the *an-arche* is summed up in the first two paragraphs of an unlikely source—"Sports of the Times":

On Broadway, in Manhattan, the center of the music industry, the construction workers slouch on their lunch hour, leering at women who do not wear brassieres, sneering at men with long hair, eyeing the sandals and boots, and dashikis and the bell bottoms and the leather vests.

With such a sideshow passing by, very little attention is paid to a man in such a prosaic outfit as a yellow sweatshirt with black and white fists and the legend WE CAN MAKE IT TO-GETHER—BUDDAH RECORDS.[12]

This indeed is sport of the times. The "hard-hats" are brothers, chronologically. In attitude, however, they speak the legend of the fathers: work, respect the values of the group, take pride in individual achievement, build for the future even if it means ignoring the present and its gratification—its "grace-ification."

The *others,* the sons and daughters of seemingly different fathers and mothers, speak and show the legend a-borning, but not yet fully present: sing, dance, play, feast (as in festival), and be present (in the new vernacular: get it all together) even if it means not caring for the morrow.

The "sport," the *agon* or contest, here, was most visible at its earlier stages in the university. It is experienced now as a political crisis, a crisis of the *polis*. The crisis is one of confrontation, not conversation; of insurrection, not resurrection.

The crisis is deeper than political, however. It involves a long period of invisible and festering preparation—as long as the period from the crisis of world-view in the sixteenth and seventeenth centuries, the scientific revolution, the age of exploration and discovery of the new worlds, the American and French revolutions, the industrial, technological, and electronic revolutions of the nineteenth and twentieth centuries, the centuries when the wounds of the earlier crises became visible and undeniably hurtful in *psyche* and *polis*. At this deeper level, part of the crisis of *an-arche* is the collusion (*col* and *ludere,* to play with) and collision (*col* and *laedere,* to strike or dash together) of fathers and children. There is *collusion* insofar as the fathers must make or in some way pay for the stuff of the style of the children. There is *collision* insofar as the legends of both are in conflict. Or rather, the legend of the children, while lived, is not yet written; the legend of the fathers, while written, is no longer lived.

In this collision between the legend no longer lived and legend being lived but not yet written lies the deepest and most explosive dimension of the *agon*. This is different from the clash or battle of world-views or ideologies. A battle of world-views is a contest in which the ground rules, so to speak, are the same for the opposing sides: commitment to the view that life is truly lived only under the structuring and ordering power of some super ego-organization. The clash comes at the point where one view asserts its superiority over the other while at the same time feeling threatened by the claims of the other even though it is seen as inferior. The threat comes at the point of perhaps having to let go, to lose control: if the view, or in our terms the *legend,* is lost, swallowed up by another view or legend, then world is lost. It should be noted that what is lost is an *idea* of the world; what appears in its stead may very well be life, not just simply another idea of life. It is something like the opposing teams in a football game, after a particularly brutal "play," sitting down on the turf and talking to each other, conversing, hearing from one another. The fans wouldn't like it, the television networks would probably sue the team owners, the TV viewers would switch to another channel: for all parties of the disaffected their "world" would have disappeared. Obviously what took its place would not be football. But neither would it be death. It would be a new expression of life.

In the collision of the legend of the fathers, not lived, and the living of the children, not written, we do not have a battle of world-views. This annoys the fathers, particularly the professorial fathers: if you cannot say it, analyze it, and explain it, then it obviously is not real. This stems from the Socratic maxim: "The unexamined life is not worth living." On the other hand, the children, at least some of them, are saying: "The unlived life is not worth examining." The life-style with which the children confront the fathers, then, is not one deduced from a system of ideas about what life *should* be. This in itself is not surprising: the fathers have long since shown the failure of systems to function in a life-giving and integrating way. The children, then, manifest an evolution of cultural-biological vitalities and present us with a whole new panoply of style: new colors, sounds, pictures, movements, words, gestures, sensations, visions, and vocabularies. In all of these we discover many ancient and honored themes: joy, playing, celebration, feasting, dancing, loving, singing, praise, fantasy, re-creation.

Here is the heart of the matter: the collision between the legends of the fathers and the lives of the children is one of vitalities. It is a collision between the *old* sensibility and the *new* sensibility. The new sensibility has been described as expressing "the ascent of the life instincts over aggressiveness and guilt." [13] The old sensibility, then, must be one of aggression and guilt: the aggression of spirit over flesh, mind over matter; and guilt at the inability to conquer the flesh. The anger of the fathers at the children is compounded: the children experience liberation which the fathers always desired but could never achieve without guilt; also, the new sensibility of the children impresses the fathers with their failure to continue and expand the powers of their own legend. Thus we experience, in the "space/time between," two challenges: a challenge of the power of body to the alleged sovereignty of mind/spirit *and* a challenge of the children to the authority of the fathers.

How is the challenge to be interpreted in terms of Christian identity? In classical Christian terms this dual challenge can be seen as a resurrection of the body from the dead and dying texts/legends of the fathers.[14] It is the reaffirmation of life in the midst of death. It is not an eternal victory of life against death: the vision of eternal life as a moment without death is false, it is "bad faith."

What I am suggesting is this: the new sensibility ("the ascent of the life instincts over aggression and guilt") is the contemporary expression of the symbol of the resurrection of the body. The problem with this is that the old legend, the old sensibility, has interpreted the resurrection of the body, as a theological and christological doctrine, in such a way as to suggest that—having "happened" once in the past—it is something that must be waited for in the future.

I remember the profound disappointment I experienced as a boy of nine or ten, at an Easter Sunday service, when it finally dawned on me what was being presented by the minister (who happened to be my father) as the "real" meaning of Christ's resurrection: namely, the resurrection of Christ's body on the long-ago first Easter morning gave me a guarantee, if I would be good, if I remained true to the commands of the Father, of eternal life. The disappointment registered at several levels: first of all, I *knew,* though hardly anyone had ever talked to me about it, that I would, in fact, die. The promise of eternal life seemed like a lie. Second: the windows of the church were open (this was in the little village of Etna in northeastern Indiana), and I could smell the spring smells, and hear the birds singing and the flies buzzing, and feel a cool draft of air. I could see beyond the barn in back of the parsonage to a field, on the far boundary of which was a stream. Along this stream grew a tree. I could climb that tree and see what seemed to be forever. I wanted to be there at that moment and experience the freeness, and fresh- ness, and clarity of that place. I was not interested in waiting for life in some far-distant future: life was beckoning, it was there all around, and I wanted it now. But I sat and listened to the rest of the legend and looked at the new hat my mother was wearing and wondered why it was so important for women to have new hats at Eastertime and was glad she did have one, since it seemed to be so important and since most of the other women in the church had new hats. Some of them even had new dresses.

The resurrection of the body: the re-eroticization of life. God the Father is not a gigantic phallus, organizing the world around his Will. He releases himself so every man and woman can feel anew the original elements of fire, air, water, and earth. The resurrection of the body is the triumph of polymorphism over genital organization. There is no object, no point, to the Incarna- tion except to release man into the field of play—enjoyment, enthusiasm. God resurrects himself as man re-experiences him- self as body. *Image dei:* man as pro-creator.

The resurrection of the body: the new sensibility, "the ascent of life instincts," the re-eroticization of life. This is where the old sensibility is challenged at its most sensitive level. The old sensibility—the old legend, the old "testament": testament is "a formal declaration, usually in writing, of a person's wishes as to the disposal of his property after his death." [15] Hence the new sensibility, the new legend, the new testament (I can find it in no dictionary): a declaration of independence from the text, usually in singing, dancing, and praising, of a person's wishes as to the disposal of his energies during his life.

The new sensibility, the new testament, the resurrection of the body: this is to experience life once again as pleasurable, satisfying, reconciling and redemptive now, not later. The physiological structure of man is that of neo-nate: he retains the newborn state throughout his life. No hair covers his body: he remains exposed to all the stimuli of his environment. Culture is a regression: it says put on clothes so you can do your work. Put on clothes—clothes of animal hide (hide is *to hide*) and vegetable stuff—identify yourself with, hide yourself in, the previous epoch so that you will not be subjected without defense to the incredible array of stimuli with which the universe bombards you.

The new sensibility, the resurrection of the body, brings back, reaffirms, the neo-nate dynamics of the human species. Resurrection is rebirth: rebirth is the removal of all defenses, sublimations and clothings, intellectual and material. To learn the secret we must be present again as body. Jesus said it in the new sensibility (the new testament): "It is easier for a camel to go through the eye of a needle, than for a rich man to enter into the Kingdom of God" (Mark 10:20, A.V.). Of course, the rich man is no neo-nate: he has too many clothes; he is muffled, so he cannot know the ecstasy. Before that Jesus also said: ". . . whosoever shall not receive the Kingdom of God as a little child, he shall not enter therein" (Mark 10:15, A.V.). Of course, the child has not built up his sublimatory defenses, he has no clothes: the child is the emperor without clothes. He receives messages the rich man cannot *feel!*

"Christian identity on today's campus?" It is the resurrection of the body, the new sensibility, the new testament. But there is still no word, no conversation, no hearing from one another. The new sensibility has not yet issued in a naming of the heavenly ones. There is singing, dancing, praising: but it remains still at the level of revelry, not a "foursome-ing," not a conversation in which the heavenly ones are named.

Here is the point at which the genius of Christian identity truly reveals itself. The word becomes flesh so that it might be transubstantiated. The word becomes flesh so that the old spirit of the unconscious may now become conscious. The word becomes flesh so that it may be resurrected and assume a place at the right hand of the Father, become co-equal and consubstantial. Two references might help: Kazantzakis and Rilke. First, Kazantzakis:

> Two violent contrary winds, one masculine and the other feminine, met and clashed at a crossroads. For a moment they counterbalanced each other, thickened, and became visible.
> This crossroads is the universe. This crossroads is my heart.
> This dance of the gigantic erotic collision is transmitted from the darkest particle of matter to the most spacious thought.[16]

And again Kazantzakis:

> . . . tell me all that you've seen on earth, all that you've
>   heard,
> and I shall pass them through my entrails' secret forge
> till slowly, with profound caresses, play and laughter,
> stones, water, fire, and earth shall be transformed into
>   spirit,
> and the mud-winged and heavy soul, freed of its flesh,
> shall like a flame serene ascend and fade in sun.[17]

Earth does not become *earth* until a praising consciousness appears. Without the praising consciousness all remains silent, unspoken. But the word becomes flesh, "dwells amongst us." The poet Hölderlin says: "Full of merit, and yet poetically, dwells Man on this earth."

The poet Rainer Maria Rilke:

. . . Are we, perhaps, here just for saying: House, Bridge, Fountain, Gate, Jug, Olive tree, Window—possibly: Pillar, Tower? . . . but for saying, remember, oh, for such saying as never the things themselves hoped so intensely to be. . . .[18]

The possibility of conversation resides in the things—those realities that gather together all of the elements and make it possible to say. But even this is not enough. So Rilke continues at the closing of the Ninth Elegy:

Earth, isn't this what you want: an invisible   2
re-arising in us? Is it not your dream
to be one day invisible? Earth! Invisible!
What is your urgent command if not transformation! [19]

The word become flesh—"the mud-winged and heavy soul" —has a destiny: to be resurrected, reborn once again into spirit, but spirit now born of conversation so that the invisible, silent ones become present once again. The word becomes flesh so that it is possible to *say,* to name the things. But the destiny of the word become *flesh,* which makes saying possible, is to be resurrected again as body-spirit, to turn saying into *conversation.* The process here is not unlike that revealed by the Zen Master who said: "Before I was enlightened the rivers were rivers, the mountains were mountains; while *seeking,* the mountains were no longer mountains, the rivers were no longer rivers; after experiencing enlightenment, once again the mountains were mountains and the rivers were, once again, rivers."

For the rivers to become not-rivers, and the mountains to become not-mountains, the word must (in our vocabulary) become flesh: we can *say* mountain, river, or jug, pillar, and know that the word is not the thing. But when the body is resurrected then the thing again becomes what it is. The difference between before enlightenment and after is the difference between incarnation and resurrection: incarnation is the word become not-word; resurrection is the body become word once again.

In the resurrection of the body lies the possibility of "naming the heavenly ones." The body resurrected becomes the heavenly one who reigns over all; earth is transformed into world, saying is transformed into conversation, and man is completed. This is the destiny of Christian identity on today's campus, as I see it; and it proceeds out of the *arche* of Christian symbolism. The secret lies in the clue already suggested: the new sensibility is the beginning of the resurrection of the body. The meaning of Christian identity is to see that this beginning is consummated in the naming of the heavenly ones. But this naming, issuing from saying, completed in conversation, begins in the resurrection of the body. Kazantzakis says it this way:

> . . . if we all desire it intensely, if we organize all the visible and invisible powers of earth and fling them upward, if we all battle together like fellow combatants eternally vigilant—then the Universe might possibly be saved.
>
> It is not God who will save us—it is we who will save God, by battling, by creating, and by transmuting matter into spirit.[20]

"Ask, and it shall be given you; seek, and ye shall find. . . ." To raise the question of Christian identity, in any context, is to say that it is lost, absent, eclipsed, destroyed. But, at the same time, to recognize the absence of Christian identity is also to recognize its presence.

It is only when you seek it that you lose it.
You cannot take hold of it, nor can you get rid of it;
while you can do neither, it goes on its own way.
You remain silent and it speaks; you speak and it is silent.[21]

This dialectic is exhibited also in Plato's *Meno:* How are we to seek for anything? If we know it, it is therefore present and there is no need to seek for it. But if we do not know it, we do not know what it is we are seeking. Pascal says the same thing in a variation on a theme of Augustine: "Console thyself, thou wouldst not be seeking me if thou hadst not already found me." The poet Hölderlin, in his late poem "Homecoming," picks up the same theme: "That which thou seekest is already near and coming to greet thee." Jesus, also, says: "The Kingdom of God is in your midst."

The point is this: the question of Christian identity is inevitably dialectic. Where the Christian Yea is strongest, the Nay manifests itself most powerfully. When the Christian Nay is strongest then the Yea is revealed. The presupposition of this essay has been that we are in the midst of a colossal Christian Nay that shows itself as an unrecognized Yea: the emergence of the new sensibility, the "ascent of the life instincts," the resurrection of the body. It is so close we neither cognize nor recognize. It is so simple it is incomprehensible.

It is too bright and so it is difficult to see.
There was a man who looked for a fire with a lighted
    lantern.
Had he known what fire was he could have cooked his
    rice much sooner.

Jesus said the same thing, differently: "Ask, and it shall be given you; seek, and ye shall find; knock, and it shall be opened unto you: for everyone that asketh receiveth; and he that seeketh findeth; and to him that knocketh it shall be opened" (Matt. 7:7–8, A.V.).

1. Norman O. Brown, *Love's Body* (New York: Random House, 1966), p. 193.
2. *Ibid.*, p. 195.
3. Nietzsche, *Thus Spake Zarathustra* (I.7), in *The Philosophy of Nietzsche* (New York: Modern Library Edition, 1954), pp. 40–41.
4. *Ibid.*, p. 39.
5. Norman O. Brown, "Apocalypse: The Place of Mystery in the Life of the Mind," in Stanley R. Hopper and David L. Miller (eds.), *Interpretation: The Poetry of Meaning* (New York: Harcourt, Brace & World, 1967), p. 11. The Emerson statement is from *Nature, Addresses, and Lectures* (Boston: Houghton, Mifflin and Co., 1894), pp. 90–91.
6. This is a paraphrase of a statement by Martin Heidegger in his essay "Hölderlin and the Essence of Poetry": ". . . in the act of establishing the essence of poetry [Hölderlin] first determines a new time. It is the time of the gods that have fled *and* of the god that is coming. It is the time of *need* because it lies under a double lack and a double Not: the No-more of the gods that have fled and the Not-yet of the god that is coming." Martin Heidegger, *Existence and Being*. With an introduction by Werner Brock (Chicago: Henry Regnery Co., 1949), p. 313.
7. Wallace Stevens, "Anecdote of the Jar," *The Collected Poems of Wallace Stevens* (New York: Alfred A. Knopf, 1967).
8. See the entry "gerund" in Partridge, *Origins: A Short Etymological Dictionary of Modern English* (New York: The MacMillan Co., 2nd ed., 1959).
9. Heidegger, *op. cit.*, pp. 300–301.
10. See Heidegger, *Vorträge und Aufsätze* (Pfullingen, Neske, 1954), pp. 170–78. For interpretations in English see also: Vincent Vycinas, *Earth and Gods* (The Hague: M. Nijhoff, 1961), p. 17 and Chap. III. William J. Richardson, *Heidegger: Through Phenomenology to Thought* (The Hague: M. Nijhoff, 1963), pp. 570–72. Richardson translates *Gevierte* as "Quadrate."
11. Alan Watts, *Does it Matter? Essays on Man's Relation to Materiality* (New York: Pantheon, 1970), pp. 29–30.
12. George Vecsey, "That's Show Biz," *New York Times*, August 12, 1970, p. 46. Mr. Vecsey's article centers on the fame and fortune of

Ed Charles since leaving the New York Mets, for whom he played 3rd base in their championship year of 1969. Mr. Charles now works as a sales representative for Buddah Records in New York City.

13. Herbert Marcuse, *Essay on Liberation* (Boston: Beacon Press, 1969), p. 23. The complete sentence reads as follows: "The new sensibility, which expresses the ascent of the life instincts over aggressiveness and guilt, would foster, on a social scale, the vital need for the abolition of injustice and misery and would shape the further evolution of the 'standard of living.' "

14. In what follows I am deeply indebted to Norman O. Brown, though beyond this acknowledgment I will not cite him. His book *Love's Body* has already been referred to in this essay. Also of utmost importance is his earlier book, *Life against Death* (Middletown: Wesleyan University Press, 1959). See especially Chap. XVI, "The Resurrection of the Body."

15. *The Oxford Universal Dictionary on Historical Principles,* revised and edited by C. T. Onions. Third edition, revised with addenda (Oxford: Clarendon Press, 1944, 1955).

16. Nikos Kazantzakis, *The Saviors of God: Spiritual Exercises.* Trans. with an introduction by Kimon Friar (New York: Simon and Schuster, 1960), p. 123.

17. Nikos Kazantzakis, *The Odyssey: A Modern Sequel.* Trans. with introduction, synopsis, and notes by Kimon Friar (New York: Simon and Schuster, a Clarion Book, 1958), the Prologue, lines 25–28. I am indebted to my former colleague, Prof. Joseph Blenkinsopp, now at the University of Notre Dame, for introducing me to these dimensions of the work of Kazantzakis. See his essay, "Kazantzakis: A Voice for the Seventies?" published in *Commonweal* in the Fall of 1970.

18. Rainer Maria Rilke, *Duino Elegies.* Trans., introduction, and commentary by J. B. Leishman and Stephen Spender (New York: W. W. Norton & Co., 1939), the Ninth Elegy, p. 75.

19. *Ibid.,* p. 77.

20. Nikos Kazantzakis, *The Saviors of God,* p. 106.

21. Cited in Alan Watts, *The Meaning of Happiness,* 2nd ed., (New York: Harper & Row, Perennial Library, 1970), p. vi.

VI

John Snow:

"The chaplain's only authority is the immediate pragmatic value of his observation. . . . The Church will again be a major shaping force in the institutional life of the West to the extent that it becomes an institution which seems to have a vision of reality which is accepted by its own members and acted upon as reality by them."

THE issue of a chaplain's religious identity in a secular institution is a matter of some consequence not only for the chaplain himself but for the institution as well. I have noticed a kind of polite curiosity and professed confusion on the part of professors and administrative people as to the religious significance of chaplains. They wonder, always politely, not what the chaplain is doing, but what the religious significance of what he's doing might be.

Actually, Dean of the Chapel, the official ceremonial religious commander in chief, is the most easily understood religious role on a university campus. He marries and buries and blesses various academic occasions with his official presence and prayers and fits comfortably into the classical traditions of the "Great Ivy League University." Until the classical traditions themselves, now in parlous state and questioned on every side, fall into final ruin, the university *qua* institution will accept the religious role of the Chapel deans as self-evident. Their problems are their own private agonies of doubt, their own internal tensions, not their public role which has a clear religious definition. The Chapel dean puts his theological energy into maintaining his selfhood and integrity in the iron grip of his institutionally defined religious role.

The same of course is not true of denominational chaplains. Even those chaplains who are happiest with their own religious role-definition and feel that their "thing" is significant theologically, often have trouble making this significance understandable to the university community which continues to have the Chapel dean as its model for a religious presence in the university. The significance of the model is ceremonial.

The average professor imagines that the denominational chaplain "does a lot of counseling," "is a very busy man," "is a pastor to his denominational flock," but then politely inquires about "religious interest" among undergraduates, asks "How many Episcopalians take an active part in religion these days?" etc., and generally evidences skepticism as to the "religious effectiveness" of the denominational chaplain.

I have noticed that where the chaplain has a major commitment to political activism, the very professors and students who work with him day in and day out and have great affection and respect for him, are still puzzled about his relationship to religion or, indeed, to Christianity. Assuming that the chaplain himself has a theological justification for his activities with which he himself feels comfortable, he nevertheless may meet with that blank gaze of polite disbelief and embarrassment even from his friends when he attempts to expound upon it. There is always the suspicion in the mind of the totally secularized individual, particularly the academic intellectual, that if a chaplain is not actively trying to convert his secular cohorts to a traditional, indeed an orthodox, Christian commitment, he is either kidding himself about his own faith or consciously putting on the Church to free him to follow some political or psychotherapeutic vocation which he has chosen for himself out of despair for Christianity. The other day a faculty revolutionary, a sociologist, suddenly looked me straight in the eye and said, "Isn't your problem that Christianity has no credible content whatsoever?" But the look in his eyes showed clearly that he was making a statement, not asking for an answer. He was convinced, preconvinced, that his assumption was true, and he was not going to give time and attention to any defense I might make of the significant content of Christianity.

It is, then, the constant attrition of being among people trapped in an ironclad empirical view of reality which is the peculiar cross of the college chaplain, and his greatest temptation is slowly to yield to this view of reality, first, in order simply to relate to the community in which he moves, and then to defend his sophistication, the excellence of his education, or, as Bill

Cosby puts it, to be cool. The simple fact of the matter is that if the chaplain does not speak the language of the university, the university is not interested in what he has to say. And so he must speak this language. But since this language is the product of a world-view, is indeed, as Donald Cutler so perceptively puts it, the language of the religion of the university, the chaplain is constantly engaged in heresy. The university demands the death of God as the basic assumption upon which its teaching rests, and it is not surprising that a death-of-God theology emerged from the academy.

Thus the college chaplain must in a sense find a theological justification for the heresy which is the condition of his simple survival in the university. This is a complicated way of saying that he must live in considerable inner tension, forgoing the temptation to accept the heresy as his religion, yet avoiding the final alienation from the community which an eyeball-to-eyeball confrontation with the religion of the university would certainly entail.

One has to take seriously Cutler's questioning of the real value of a chaplain's presence in the university, and this questioning is certainly shared by members of the institutional Church outside the university. They, like many of the academic community itself (who may be active members of the institutional Church, like parish vestrymen, delegates to general conventions, etc.), are also suspicious that the chaplain is putting them on. How quick the institutional Church is to dispense with these chaplaincies when money gets tight is an indication of its latent distrust of their value. This adds to the inner tension of the chaplain, and makes the issue of his religious identity even more important.

So here is the chaplain, usually not assaulted from all sides, since, if he keeps his nose clean he is not regarded as a menace, but existing in an atmosphere of mild distrust, generally regarded as more of a fool than a knave by those who don't know him, with his support usually based on his charm, his intelligence, or his usefulness to the university rather than on any felt understanding of his religious significance. It is not a healthy situation psychologically, and it requires a certain inner sureness in a man about the importance, not of his job, but of Christianity itself. Having so few props, so few built-in assurances of the significance of his role, the chaplain is thrown back upon the content of Christianity in order to find his vocation. Thus one vocation, for a chaplain in a university, and one which is seldom claimed, is to be a theologian. This means that his primary concern is not the university at all, but to serve the Church.

Within the university he is not a subversive but a sort of benign spy. The university is his adversary but not his enemy. In a way he must love it, really care about what it does, respect the men who are so deeply committed to its enterprise, because the university tolerates him, is open to him, and provides him freely with its services. It gives him a place to work and the justification for a house and salary. It keeps his mind sharp, provides him with a great deal of data that he needs, and often with a congregation and a place to conduct worship. But his priestly and pastoral functions are not terribly demanding if the university counseling services are adequate. His congregation is ferociously busy with its studies, its social life, its sports, its political involvements, with the endless experimentation of youth. Its physical health is superb. There are few marriages and fewer funerals. There are few substantive things the chaplain can teach that the Department of Religion can't teach better. If he has great interpersonal gifts he may eventually find a curious role of ombudsman among the faculty and administration, but even this role is most significant in the opportunity it provides for observation and learning.

For we must make no mistake, the university is where the

mind-set of each new generation of national leadership is completed. It, and not the Church, is what provides the final arena for men and women to work out their value systems, learn the skills necessary to follow their vocations, come to grips with the latest ideological trends, and discover their individual styles of interpersonal relationship. This takes place, to use Cutler's phrase, within the religion of the university, that is, with certain assumptions implicit in the institution which mightily influence the thought and action of the generations educated there.

Someone in the Church should be aware of what is going on in the universities and interpreting it to the Church, along with its implications for Christian theology. The old truism about how people with a good Christian background will give up religion in college and then inevitably return to Church when they marry and have children is not likely to hold unless the Church speaks from some understanding of what went into the education of this generation and is able to cross the enormous communications gap that currently exists and will probably widen in the next decade. The strong possibility exists that more and more of those young men and women who graduate from college four years from now will neither marry nor have children. They are learning in the universities today that the traditional Christian monogamous family is an ecological menace, contributing to the competitive consumption of the earth's limited supplies, contributing to overpopulation, and failing to provide an adequate community to overcome the increasing alienation and mental illness of human society. What will the Church have to say to people who seek no blessing for their liaisons, whose children will be communally parented if they have children, and who have become increasingly distrustful of any language in their worship, preferring silence or communal chanting or dancing? These things are not likely to vanish. Indeed, as the population continues to increase catastrophically so will experimentation in communal life, so will experimentation in genetic engineering. So, most probably, will man's whole understanding of who he is change radically. In some cases it will be the Church's responsibility to adapt and in others to resist with all its heart. But who is thinking about this horrendously rapid change in values and life-styles in Christian terms, presently? And where can it be done but in the universities which are producing it?

Immediately it comes to mind that the chaplain's role should have something to do with the shaping of the academic arena, that the chaplain should be outspoken about the value assumptions which saturate his role, and in many instances outspokenly critical; but again this assumes that someone would listen to him. I suspect at this point that the theology of chaplains tends to be so idiosyncratic, so individualized, that it has little or no authority when it is applied to institutions. Harry Stack Sullivan's definition of reality (that which is consensually validated) is an assumption of the religion of the university, and not only does the theology of an individual chaplain find little consensual validation within the university, it finds little consensual validation within the institutional Church, either. Speaking for himself, the chaplain's only authority is the immediate pragmatic value of his observation. He may be valued for the shrewdness of his observations on the university scene, but not for their theological profundity. To the extent that the Church will ever again be a major shaping force in the institutional life of the West, it will be as a total institution which seems to have a vision of reality that is largely accepted by its own members, and acted upon as reality by them.

Margaret Mead maintains that the salvation of the earth, the planet, will depend on developing a religion which has science at its heart. Although she has not yet volunteered to be crucified and rise from the dead in three days, we should perhaps listen to her, at least to the extent of giving close attention to Teilhard de Chardin and realizing that we shall never again be able to communicate with any significant numbers of human beings if we fail to admit liturgically and theologically that reality is not static but process. This, as Teilhard notes, does not throw us into any major conflict with the Bible, but only with the curiously enduring judicial analogies of Anselmian theology that became frozen into our liturgies and theology during the High Middle Ages. Reality as an everlasting courtroom scene, though suddenly full of ironic relevance for the college dean and perhaps generally for the nation during the next decade, the decade of the trial as prophesied by the Chicago conspirators, is nevertheless not an adequately defined reality to help build a world which is a home for man, and over which Christ would deign to be called King.

There is, then, a crying need for a theological consensus within the Church which takes into consideration the trends now brewing in the universities in the society to come. It should be underlined that these trends are not the only ones which will be shaping these institutions. The Church if it gets itself together theologically could become a significant force in the social restructuring which is to come. So will urban political coalitions emerging from the crisis in the cities be strong shaping forces, but it should be added that these forces, from the Panthers to progressive young party politicians, tend to proselytize the universities and to be heard there constantly, so that the chaplain is not altogether out of touch with their thinking or their activities, nor does his work keep him from some urban involvement. Another potentially shaping force, the counter-culture, is always observable on a university campus.

I mention all this because I'm anticipating the argument that Departments of Religion are a sufficient theological presence in the universities. I truly wish they were, but my limited experience leads me to believe that nowhere does the religion of the university hold stronger sway than in those departments. At Princeton it is a policy that no member of the Department of Religion participates in any enterprise of the United Christian Ministry because such participation damages the department's claim to objectivity and its professional status in the university. The Department of Religion is big and good and popular and intends to stay that way, but its obsession with what Buber calls "the cruel problematic," its disinterest in synthesis, its absence of commitment, make it an enthusiastic disciple of the religion of the university, and any theology to emerge from it will very probably be heavily influenced by this religion, whether it calls itself Christian or not.

The theologian who would have most to give, then, if one were to seek a model, would be a college chaplain, hopefully with a doctorate in theology, who has a student-faculty, or at least student, congregation, conducts regular worship, takes his pastoral responsibilities seriously, and though seeking some sacramental involvement in university or urban affairs is *primarily* concerned with doing theology. By theology I do not mean a brilliant new breakthrough into something or other, but a patient, systematic, critical synthesis of that current theology which is commanding large blocks of universal understanding and agreement—Teilhard, Moltmann, Gilkey, and the whole new flowering of Roman Catholic theology since Vatican II. If there were ten or fifteen such men holding college chaplaincies, sharing the theological task and in constant close communication with one another, given their task by the authority of the major denominations and funded by them, the college chaplaincy would be not only an unquestioned blessing to the institutional Church, but a slowly growing force in the university itself.

This model is something for the future, but it is not altogether irrelevant when we try to deal with the immediate issue of the chaplain's religious identity, with what is going on in his head and heart that makes him feel that his Christian vocation is fast disappearing by osmosis into the religion of the university. At this point I must describe my own chaplaincy, how I deal with my own Christian identity after nearly two years as a chaplain at Princeton University.

Very quickly I moved the Sunday service from 9:00 A.M. to 10:00 P.M., which proved to have many advantages that I didn't calculate at the time. For the first time in many years I was able to become a parishioner in a large Episcopal Church and worship with my family. All of us, wife and children, became active in the parish and found much of our life there. As it turned out, the parish was one of the few points where town and gown met, so that my introduction to faculty was more through the parish than through the university. I found myself serving on committees, giving children's sermons, occasionally preaching at the regular Sunday services, and addressing various groups in the Church. This led to preaching engagements and lectures at other parishes within the area and beyond. Thanks to planes, I can usually get back for my own late evening services. The preaching and speaking became an exercise in theological experimentation: trying to reduce parts of Teilhard to communicable material for luncheon groups; introducing to large, mixed congregations certain significant aspects of current university trends and submitting them to radical theological criticism—and getting feedback at the discussion periods which followed. My strategy, at this early period of a year or two in the job, is to see what the parish can bear intellectually; to probe into the silent majority, looking for interstices in its conformist defenses, and trying to see how much, by traditional biblical language and dialogue used carefully and accurately, I can convey of a process theology within an eschatological framework, which is where I think theology will have to go.

All of this, for me, has meant minimal involvement in the university itself beyond my involvement with Episcopal students. I see a lot of them, informally and in counseling, and preach to around eighty students who attend services with a degree of regularity. My religious identity is very much fed by the worship, the preaching, the felt sense of Christian community which we have as a small congregation in the midst of a large secular institution that hardly notices us. I try to make this community a place where students can stand off from their university involvement and examine it from a Christian perspective unavailable elsewhere. I am aware that this chaplaincy as it has taken shape is very unlike most current chaplaincies, but I am increasingly convinced that it is meeting a felt need of students as part of their "strategy of survival in a permanently apocalyptic world" (to misquote Susan Sontag). It is they as much as I who have shaped it this way and our mutual need for strengthening our Christian identities is served by it. I would add that three out of perhaps six key students coordinating and shaping the "strike" at Princeton in the spring of 1970 were faithful members of this Christian community.

Thus, if I pull together the ingredients of my chaplaincy which contribute to my Christian identity I think it would come out like this: my participating membership with my family in a parish; my experimental attempts by preaching and lecturing outside the university to identify major trends in university thought and value and submit them to theological criticism in a grass-roots milieu where there is instant feedback; my traditional role as priest and pastor to Episcopal students; the regular weekly preaching of the gospel, where I try to maintain an ongoing reflection on the life and thought of the university in the light of the gospel.

In this last function of the traditional ministry I find my own inner spiritual life. Monday morning I read carefully the propers for the following Sunday. I then take the Bible and carefully read the full context of the Gospel and the Epistle passages appointed, and when something grabs me I read whatever commentary I have available on it. From then on, as the week progresses, I free-associate to all this material. I try to keep my eyes open and look for signs. I try to notice what is going on—by reading the campus newspaper; by attending rallies, demonstrations, lectures, etc., and by talking talking talking with faculty and students. All the while, in the back of my mind the Scripture is percolating, until the Spirit moves me and I can write a sermon. It will always have as its text the Proper collect, or a passage from the Epistle or Gospel for the day. Over the years I've found the Bible an extraordinarily rich source of what I can only call "life." Its relevance continues to obsess me and, in no small way, to give me hope.

There is a final ingredient of the chaplaincy which for me is the most demanding, difficult, and important of all, and lies at the heart not of my Christian identity but of the expression of this identity in vocation: namely, those two months off in the summer when I feel I'm called to get it all together for the Church. One summer it was the Kellogg Lectures. Currently it is a joint endeavor with others to sweat out a theological approach to ecology for the National Council of Churches. I think I find this part of my vocation difficult because of my woeful lack of specialized preparation for doing theology, my total lack of expertise in philosophy, and a natural abhorrence for abstraction. This is why I think it is so important for Doctors of Theology to be chaplains—because the demands of the job keep them honest and involved, but not so involved that there is no time for their special craft.

After ten years of parish militancy, deep involvement in the movement, utter engrossment in urban problems with the endless committee work, I find day after day of solitude with a typewriter trying to dredge up old skills and learn new ones a very taxing business, especially when I know the results will be a good deal less than they ought to be. But for me, in this moment in history, not to do this is to waste an opportunity given to few clergymen, to give some help to the Church where it needs help most, and to provide, for my own chaplaincy at least, the sense of a truly Christian vocation.

VII

Paul E. Schrading:

"The problem of authenticity can be understood more clearly when one has a sense of inwardness and piety. If I can be at peace with myself and remain open to the present and the future, the problem of being authentic will not readily plague me."

I. THE words of Ugo Betti on the Corita Kent print—"To believe in God is to know that all the rules will be fair and that there will be wonderful surprises."—provide a context for understanding the meaning of Christian identity on today's campus. The university is undergoing significant change in purpose and direction. Previously assumed relationships of the university to society are seriously questioned. The rate of change is vigorously debated. Some feel our institutions of higher education are too readily influenced by the critics, while others claim that universities are bastions of a decaying culture. The dynamics of change, however, are evident in every institution.

The struggle for Christian identity in higher education is part of this changing pattern. The university setting, among others in our culture, is clearly part of our post-Christian era. By post-Christian I mean that our relationships within structures and our common assumptions are no longer formed by reference to the Christian cultural heritage. Liberal learning and liberal politics shared a common vision of man the maker, molding a future based upon a progression of ideals drawn from the Christian cultural heritage. Serious believers in the Christian faith were quick to point out the ironies of American history or the glorification of Christian symbols for narrow national and parochial causes. Historically, the dropping of the A-bomb on Hiroshima in August of 1945 may serve as that event which confronted the liberal assumptions of nation and church, and thrust us into the post-Christian era. From that period the United States developed a posture of world influence, interlocking cultural, economic, military, and educational interests which challenged the liberal assumptions of our heritage. The imagery of man the maker had turned into man the manipulator for his own causes.

We still have examples of the close ties between national interest and the churchly empire; Billy Graham helps sponsor an

Honor America Day and the churches are reluctant to question the use of their investments in multinational corporations which gain large profit from the low wages and inhumane treatment of people in such countries as Angola and Brazil. The relationship of Christendom and the national state will continue, but the post-Christian era has opened up new possibilities for evaluation and critique.

Thus it is possible that the struggle for Christian identity on today's campus can be open to the wonderful surprises of faith. The calcification of much of the history of the relationship between church and state can be criticized openly.

II. In relation to Christian identity on the campus, we are not searching for a Paradise Lost. The university has never been a location for the gathering of Christian clans. In spite of the public relations of denominational headquarters and the ill-fated "return to religion" of the 1950s, the search for Christian faithfulness in university life has always been among a small minority. This needs to be emphasized, because many people today feel we are losing something that was a vital part of the campus scene.

Historically, the campus ministry has always been involved with small groups of students and faculty, relative to the size of the college or university. We must not be tempted to play the "numbers game."

Christian identity involves much more than counting students at worship or asking them their religious preference. It involves a commitment in faith, a pattern of community life, an ethical posture and an ability to communicate the thought processes of faith. These factors are much more difficult to measure and weigh. Christian identity, then, is extremely hard to assess in objective terms.

Before we can examine some factors of Christian identity it is necessary to explore further the context in which faith can be meaningful and vital. The new militants and neomystics on the contemporary campus are struggling to define assumptions and life-styles which have religious implications; the effort to find the holy amidst the mundane; the search for a meaningful vocation; the campaign to address the pressing issues of our time. We cannot readily baptize these efforts as Christian; to do so would be as disastrous for our faith as the baptism of national goals. Nor can we ignore their struggle for religious meaning in our understanding of the Christian faith.

III. Krister Stendahl, dean of the Harvard Divinity School, indicates there is a crisis of faith in the current understanding of campus ministry.[1] This crisis of faith, however, permeates every level and structure of the Church. The crisis comes when the old structures for theological reflection and the old structures of churchly empire are no longer relevant to the needs and concerns of the present and future. The death-of-God debate fizzled because the diverse arguments were aimed at old structures which already had crumbled. The ecumenical energy leading toward COCU (Consultation on Church Union) will probably wane because of a lack of genuine interest in revising old structures.

The crisis of faith is accentuated on the university campus because of the increased activity of the young and their moral concern for participation and priorities. In fact, much of the pursuits for integrity, peace, future possibilities, and new patterns are positive results of the breakdown of old structures. A crisis does not always imply that there will be negative results.

Several problems of our society come into bold relief because of the crisis of faith. If we can resolve these, and other problems, perhaps the present crisis of the time will be looked back upon as a genuine *kairos,* the right time for the new to emerge.

The Problem of Hypocrisy: Before our very eyes the myths of American democracy have been exposed: the myth of equality, the myth of civilian control of the military, the myth of support for oppressed people, the myth of benevolent capitalism. The taken-for-granted world in politics, economics, education, and religion is questioned.

The Problem of Manipulation: More of our citizens and many of our students are now convinced that might does not make right. Vietnam and Cambodia are ample proof. For the post-1945 children, the United States was a dominant power, and a power exercising military and economic control over many areas of the world. This is quite in contrast to the image presented by the pre-1940 United States, whose posture was isolation and disengagement. Thus, the college student today fears, or is at least concerned about, the manipulative power of his own government over his life and the lives of many others around the world. Students see a new need for flexibility in education but often cannot even make an appointment with a major professor because he is too busy elsewhere (perhaps in government research). They are the TV children, after all, who know the power of the "Marlboro Man" and the "You've come a long way, woman," and know that cancer will result. If, as some charge, the new radicals are manipulative in their techniques with groups and crowds, perhaps we should recognize that they have learned some lessons well from their fathers in industry, government, and the Church.

The Problem of Authenticity: How do we search for some personal identity in the midst of *anomie,* apathy, fear, hopelessness, and shyness about faith? Religious surrogates are easy to find in pills, pot, and panaceas, but problems relating to meaning and community are ever present. Theodore Roszak, in his book *The Making of a Counter-Culture,* suggests that many of the brightest and most gifted among the young have been horrified and revolted by the cruelties of an order which sees itself as pragmatic, reasonable, realistic, and scientific. In order to be human, many conclude they must reject these components of culture and find authentic identity through subjective rather than objective means—drugs, mysticism, and horoscopes. The search for authenticity is perhaps even more prevalent on campus than in the early years of the 1950s when there was a trend for students to be searching for true identity in the self.

These problems are not easily solved for individuals or communities. However, the struggle to understand our Christian faith must be seen in relation to these problems. Awareness of hypocrisy may lead us to examine the presuppositions of our faith, to determine more existentially the place of the Christ event in our life, and to be prepared constantly to attack the false gods which contest for our commitment. Awareness of manipulation may direct our attention more clearly to the actions of our own lives and those of the communities with which we associate. The search for authenticity may force us constantly to explore our own life-styles and religious sensitivities.

The current cultural setting of the university and the crises of faith are part of our own informing history. It is important for us to attempt to tell our own story in relation to our time. What are the factors of Christian identity in the current university setting?

IV. *Commitment with Iconoclasm:* Commitment in faith is a profound factor in the identity of the Christian, especially if it is balanced with a radical iconoclasm. The commitment stance of the Christian is confessional. Rational arguments, reliance upon authorities, and emotional preaching may have their place. "Who do you say that I am?" is the question disciples in all ages must face. The Christian begins with a reference point in Christ; neither reducing the event of Christ to the good man as an example nor explaining everything by an elevated Christocentrism. I confess that my way of thinking about myself, my companions, and our common destiny is shaped and molded by the event of God's love for man and his hope for man evidenced in Jesus Christ. The friendship between God and man is established in a new way by reference to the Christ of faith. H. Richard Niebuhr expresses the critical relationship of Christ to confessing faith in a simple and yet profound way: "Jesus Christ is for me, as for many of my fellow Christians, the one who lived and died and rose again for this cause of bringing God to men and men to God and so also of reconciling men to each other and to their world." [2]

Niebuhr goes on to say that "the establishment of this friendship is to me the key problem in human existence." This confessional faith is not only a mark of religious identity, but also the very key to understanding our human identity. How can this be proved, examined, measured by the contemporary and critical university rationalism? Perhaps the new mood of testing reality by feeling and affirmation as well as by reason will give us a key to the stance of the Christian. Perhaps our rational epistemologies need to be examined again. The confessional stance of Christian identity is essential, whether it be examined from biblical, historical, psychological, or social analysis. Christian apologetics attempted to relate the stance of faith to the powerful epistemologies of each age. The "Christian *and* . . ." series still provokes us into proving the validity of the Christian faith vis-à-vis another position, and usually the arguments are laid out to win for our side. I'm not really trying to deny the rigorous attention we should give our confession of faith, for the danger is a smug recitation of cozy words. My position is, rather, that we not finally expect that our faith will be established by a superior argument, or a course in theology. Confessionally, it grabs us or it does not. In my own understanding the central factor in my Christian identity is a reference to the commanding and powerful influence of God's reconciling act in Jesus Christ. This act stands as a key to my self-understanding, without which my affirmation as a Christian means very little.

Certainly there is more to be said and many more questions can and should be asked about this confessional stance: How do I know if my relationship to Christ is more than passing fantasy? Am I not merely using the confessional stance to avoid the marks of proof? Why not affirm human existence without a transcendent reference? The attempt here is basically to affirm that the most critical factor in assessing Christian identity is an experience and a confession that the Christ event molds and shapes the way in which the Christian perceives himself, his neighbor, and his world.

The Christian affirmation, however, is balanced with a radical iconoclasm. An iconoclast is described as one who breaks or destroys images, especially those set up for religious veneration. We constantly refer to new symbols to describe the dynamic of faith, and we must recognize the danger that the symbol can become the reality. Christ the reconciler is a symbol for a dynamic relation between men and God and between man and man, but it can become, as a symbol, that which we worship.

Radical iconoclasm in the Christian context presumes a faith in the One beyond the many, a Center of Value, a reality which, by faith, is more than the symbol system used as its vehicle. Again, H. Richard Niebuhr struggled with this attempt to understand faith in God as a permanent revolution of the mind and heart: "So faith in God involves us in a permanent revolution of the mind and heart, a continuous life which opens out infinitely into ever new possibilities. It does not, therefore afford grounds for boasting but only for simple thankfulness. It is a gift of God." [3]

The commitment in faith, balanced with a radical iconoclasm, enables the Christian to face the problem of hypocrisy. The false pretenses are constantly challenged as one weighs and measures the forces that call for action and involvement. No ideal is too sacred to be challenged. No action too mundane for living out a faithful response to one's God and neighbor. The relation of the Christian to structures of power cannot be avoided; fence-sitting is not the regular stance of commitment in faith.

William Stringfellow perceived this radical iconoclasm in his book *Dissenter in a Great Society*: ". . . the Church is always authorised to complain, for the sake of this world, about everything in this world. By the mercy of God, the inherent, invariable, unavoidable, intentional, unrelenting posture of the church in the world is one of radical protest and profound dissent toward the prevailing status quo of secular society, whatever that may be at any given time, however much men boast that theirs is a great society." [4]

My confessing relation to the event of Christ, perhaps dimly perceived, is the key factor in Christian identity. The contemporary university campus is a location where belief systems mingle regularly. Campus ministers have perhaps more opportunity today to confess their faith than when the university was tied to a liberal-rational ideology that knowledge was the measure of man. Now the measure of man is more open to question and the prospects for a campus ministry more vital.

V. *Community with Parabolic Action:* Another factor of Christian identity is an involvement in a community of parabolic action. We cannot escape the challenge that our faith calls us into a community of believers. We dare not deny the private encounter with faith (going into one's own closet for prayer), but the main impact of the Judeo-Christian heritage is the call to be a people of God and to respond as a people of faith, warts and all. One danger of the current trend to "do one's own thing" is to define a response to faith in a narrow, individualistic mode. It even encourages bitterness and strife for those who respond to faith in differing ways. The solution is approached when a community of faith acts in ways that are responsive to a tradition longer than the last meeting's agenda and in ways that are creating new responses to the present and future.

A Christian community is necessary as a factor of Christian identity. We mutually share in celebrations and joy as well as in sorrow and comfort. The modes of expressing our thanksgiving, intercession, and responding to God's word in faith differ greatly. The calcified liturgies of the Reformation are being rightly challenged, and dancing and hugging are now more honestly a part of expressing our community; festival and fantasy are being revived in the celebration of community. The basic assumption of the Christian community is that we are called together by God for mutual support and for a mission of faithfulness in the world. One image of the Christian community has been the gathering and scattering image. I prefer the image of the staging area, where resources are gathered and strategy is developed for a common task.

Christian community at the university will have many different forms, and experimentation with new forms is to be encouraged. However, I believe it very important to have a diverse group, crossing the common barriers. If only radical students gather in exclusive cells, it is just as distorted as football players gathering for their prayers before the game. The struggle of faith is too important to be limited to an age category or a vocational grouping. We must demonstrate the pluralism of our involvement in faith across the barriers that too easily divide us. Perhaps the broken wall should become more a symbol of our faith: the broken wall of our rigid liturgies; the broken wall of our slavery to rationalism in religion; the broken wall of animosity between young and old, black and white, rich and poor; the broken wall of the present structures that confine and dehumanize. In short, a radical flexibility is inherent in the commitment to the Christian community.

Peter's visit with Cornelius may be instructive for us when we attempt to build the Christian community, be it a COCU church or the underground church. "What God has cleansed, you must not call common." New forms will surely be required to break through our denominationalism, moralism, and White House ceremonies. These new forms should not fall into the same exclusivist traps of the present churchly empires.

We are not just static communities, however, although many churches are little more than dots on the denominational chart. We are active and acting communities of faith. Richard Shaull spoke at the University Christian Movement, "Process 67" conference, in Cleveland, about the nature of parabolic action (living a parable); action which manifests the faith of the believer. Perhaps we should also speak of the parabolic community of faith, through whose life and style the basis of commitment is translated into observable forms, not so much to publicize the community as to demonstrate the viability of a commitment to the story of faith which describes our understanding of the human and the eternal.

Shaull spoke to a group of leaders in the Resistance and several men turned their draft cards in at the service. The parable of their lives was being acted out. I had a strange sense at the time that the mood of that service must have been similar to the early (late-nineteenth-century) missionary conferences when students came forward to evangelize the world in that generation. We can easily criticize the missionary zeal and its attachment to economic and military imperialism, but we cannot deny the imperative to live our lives so that others may see through them to the source of our faith. Resisting the draft, opposing the war, fighting pollution, and identifying with antipoverty programs have all been ways that campus Christian communities have attempted to live out their faith as a parable. There is a dynamic tension between the faith and the action. Neither is of solitary importance. Faith without involvement is a clanging symbol, and action (for the Christian) without faith is aimless busy work. We act so that we may perceive our faith as well as let others perceive it. Otherwise we would rightly be accused of putting on a show.

Christian community with parabolic action helps us overcome the problem of manipulation. We are not then easily swayed to follow after the whims of the advertisers or the self-interest of the Pentagon. In community we have the checks and balances of a pluralistic group and our actions are not elevated as final solutions. We recognize contingency and ambiguity. For this reason I have often thought that a Christian community would have a difficult time giving undivided attention to a singular revolutionary cause. The Christians should probably be shot first in a revolution because of their iconoclasm and flexibility. However just the cause, we still refuse to worship the leader and blindly follow after him.

Christian community with parabolic action is a balancing factor of Christian identity. An isolated commitment in faith can lead us to "do our thing," but an involvement in community avoids this danger. One problem of the contemporary campus among Christian groups is that those who are on the right in the political spectrum emphasize commitment and minimize communal involvements; those on the left in the spectrum emphasize community actions but often forget about the importance of commitment in faith.

VI. *Human Piety with Openness:* It is with considerable caution that we can even speak of piety in the contemporary world. The concept of piety has been systematized and routinized in all too many negative forms; habits which consume rather than release; practices which atrophy with time; attitudes which justify cruelty and gross manipulation. It is not necessary, however, to throw out a meaningful term because of its misuse. We must examine as a part of Christian identity on the campus, along with commitment in community, an attitude of prayer and inwardness, a reflection upon Scripture, and a participation in the celebration of worship. All this we call a human piety that is an essential ingredient for our life together in faith.

Henry Horn, a Lutheran university pastor in Cambridge for many years, wrote the following in reference to the need for a human piety as part of our identity as Christians: ". . . Some discipline is required to keep the Christian close to the Person whom he celebrates with his fellow Christians, and to the testimony about that person in Scripture. In other words, the bilingual character of the Christian's life must find a discipline which will keep him in contact with his homeland." [5]

In less traditional language, Father Daniel Berrigan speaks of the need for guidelines in the exercise of Christian faith. He does not refer in this passage to piety, but the chapter heading in which the following reflection is found is appropriately titled "Journey Toward Fidelity": ". . . Certain things will always endure, if change is not to become chaos. There is no need to become dogmatic here, or to compose a new chain of 'things to believe.' The real point is living faith, charity, a Christ who is present. And from the human point of view, the retention of good humor, courage, suppleness of heart, openness to conversion, inwardness. Literally everything else is worth sacrificing for these. And these cannot be sacrificed for anything else." [6]

Piety refers to our sense of reverence and awe, a characteristic of Christian identity that provides a time apart from the routine. Reflection requires time for standing apart from the crowd. Piety with openness is essential, however. So many forms of piety have closed in upon themselves because their advocates became narrow in outlook. Discipline with openness is a difficult balance to achieve, but is a characteristic of our Christian identity. The problem of authenticity can be understood more clearly when one has a sense of inwardness and piety. If I can be at peace with myself and remain open to the present and the future, the problem of being authentic will not readily plague me.

VII. The factors of Christian identity are dynamically interlocked: commitment with iconoclasm, community with parabolic action, and piety with openness. None of these can be isolated easily from the other. They balance each other. Christian identity on the campus is not much different from the struggle for Christian identity elsewhere. This is not only because the campus has become more involved in the wider community affairs, but because factors of Christianity cannot be separated into vocational camps.

Some of the early Christians were referred to as people of the way. Symbolically this is very helpful in our time, because so many Christians and churches seem more concerned about their fixed status than the mobility of faith. Some theologians have used the symbol of the exodus to describe the activity of the Christian community. Richard Shaull even suggests a strategy of guerrilla action in the present revolutionary struggle. He suggests that biblical realism "is free to see the place of conflict in society and accept it." [7] Ours is surely a society of conflict and we need some guidelines to appraise the conflict and our role in it. There is no escape for the Christian community from an involvement in resisting structures of oppression and dehumanization and in creating alternatives for creative life and faith. We will differ at times in our appraisal of what to resist and what to support; we, too, will miss the mark, as do so many of our contemporaries.

The struggles of our time are painfully apparent and we cannot afford the luxury of noninvolvement as a Christian community in efforts toward a new humanity and a new Church. We dare not, however, accept the folly that our own vision for a new society is the one we should impose upon all men.

Daniel Berrigan suggests that "One will always respect the truth of tradition, at the risk of becoming a mere destroyer. On the other hand, the Gospel nowhere urges us to remain within a decaying nest." [8]

1. Krister Stendahl, "The Professional Identity of the Campus Minister: Report on the First Consultation on the Future of the Campus Ministry," Resource Analysis (Cambridge, Mass.: Church Society for College Work 1970), p. 14.

2. H. Richard Niebuhr, *The Responsible Self* (New York: Harper & Row, 1963), p. 44.

3. H. Richard Niebuhr, *Radical Monotheism and Western Culture* (New York: Harper & Row, 1960), p. 126.

4. William Stringfellow, *Dissenter in a Great Society* (New York: Holt, Rinehart and Winston, 1966), pp. 142–143.

5. Henry E. Horn, *The Christian in Modern Style* (Philadelphia: Fortress Press, 1968), p. 166.

6. Daniel Berrigan, *Consequences: Truth and . . .* (New York: Macmillan Co., 1967), p. 5.

7. Carl Oglesby and Richard Shaull, *Containment and Change* (New York: Macmillan Co., 1967), p. 240.

8. Berrigan, *op. cit.*